The God of Glory Thunders

The God of Glory Thunders

A Christ-centred devotional exposition
of Psalm 29

Gordon Cooke

BRYNTIRION PRESS

Published by Bryntirion Press
Bryntirion, Bridgend CF31 4DX, Wales, UK
Printed by Gomer Press, Llandysul, Ceredigion SA44 4JL

To

Linda and Bethany

'I will sing to the LORD,
Because he has dealt bountifully with me.'
(Psalm 13:6)

Contents

Introduction

ABOUT five miles from where I live, there is a tourist attraction that welcomes thousands of people every year. It is a scenic drive through a beautiful area of the forestry that covers the hills and mountains of so much of the south Wales countryside. Only a few miles long, you can complete the entire drive in less than an hour. Most people, however, choose to proceed at a more leisurely pace, as at various spots there are wondrous views not just of this part of the Principality, but also over the Severn Estuary to England.

At intervals along the driveway are parking places replete with picnic tables and barbecue facilities, and in summertime these prove particularly popular. It is from these places that the driver is especially able to take in the panorama of creation on display.

The visitor who chooses to explore the scenic drive on foot, however, sees far more of the attraction than does the motorist. The pedestrian is not confined to examining it at the appointed and well-visited car parks. He will see vistas that the driver must miss, because the latter has his eyes on the narrow track! The walker is repaid the extra energy he must expend, because he sees what those confined to the picnic spots miss.

It is a little like that with the book of Psalms. Ask any Christian what their favourite Bible book is, and, chances are, they will say the Psalms. The Psalter has been an unsurpassed source of comfort and encouragement to God's people down through the ages. No matter what the circumstance of our lives, there is a psalm that speaks to it and ministers to us. But, like that scenic drive, for many people the only parts of the Psalms they ever visit are the well-known 'picnic sites'—Psalms 23, 46, 51, 100, 121, 139, and perhaps a few others. Yet in between

9

these familiar resting-places there are many glorious psalms that are virtually unknown to the majority of God's people. Those willing to walk through the Psalms will discover their beauty too!

Psalm 29 surely comes into that category. For every hundred Christians who can recite, or at least tell you what Psalm 23 is about, you will do well to find one with a similar knowledge of this psalm—one that appears, perhaps, on the next page of their Bible! Though many books have been written on the 'Shepherd Psalm', none appears to have been devoted to the 'Psalm of the Thunderstorm'. And yet many of the features which make David's most famous composition so well-loved are also found in this psalm—powerful imagery, a great view of God, descriptions of his merciful provision for his people, gospel themes later developed in the New Testament, to name just a few!

It is as an attempt to open up this wonderful psalm that this book has been written. Those who know me well will appreciate the irony of my having written it. As a child I had an intense fear, almost a phobia, about thunderstorms. Although that has diminished somewhat, they are still far from being my favourite climatic condition. Whilst my wife will happily watch a storm at night from the bedroom window, I would rather have my head underneath the pillow! Perhaps because of this, though, I have always taken an interest in the thunderstorms of the Bible, and have come to appreciate the power of this psalm particularly.

The book is subtitled 'a Christ-centred devotional exposition'. My hope is that, to quote a recent television advert, 'it does exactly what it says on the tin'. The exposition is devotional in nature, dealing with issues relating to the Hebrew text only where absolutely necessary. Anyone looking for more detailed information on these matters is referred to the commentaries named in the references throughout the book.

The book is also unashamedly Christ-centred. If, at the beginning of his earthly ministry, the Lord Jesus told us to 'search the Scriptures, for . . . these are they which testify of me', and then at its conclusion said his life and words had fulfilled 'all things . . . which were written in the Law of Moses and the Prophets and the Psalms concerning me', he must be found in Psalm 29, just as he is found in Psalm 22. My prayer is that as you meditate on this psalm you too will find him and, in doing so, have a greater view not only of a lovely psalm but also of a lovely Saviour.

Gordon Cooke
January 2006

1
The voice of the Lord

'The voice of the LORD is over the waters;
The God of glory thunders;
The LORD is over many waters.'
(Psalm 29:3)

In August 2004 a flash flood hit the small coastal village of Boscastle in the south-west of England, causing millions of pounds' worth of damage but, mercifully, no fatalities or serious injuries. A summer thunderstorm had unleashed several inches of rain upon the village in a matter of an hour, and the result was devastating.

All that evening the news broadcasts concentrated on the events of the afternoon. Video footage of vehicles floating down the main street of the village and out into the harbour were shown, alongside film of the dramatic rescue of villagers and holidaymakers from the rooftops of their homes or cars. Then the experts appeared, to explain to us how such a thing could happen. They showed us maps portraying how the village was at the confluence of two rivers, both of which had been swollen by the rain of previous days' thunderstorms, and had now broken their banks. The fact that the village was situated in a ravine, between mountainous cliffs on either side, also didn't help, as water cascaded onto the village from the steep rock formations above. All of this, no doubt, was of little consequence to the villagers, as they saw millions of gallons of rainwater, and all the debris it carried, pouring in through their front doors, and washing away their possessions, their businesses, their hopes and their dreams.

As if that wasn't enough analysis, the news broadcast was followed by the weather forecast. Using all the gadgetry at his disposal, the meteorologist showed us the satellite imagery of the storm, as it struck the Cornish coast and then headed off, to dump whatever rain it still carried on other poor, unsuspecting folk. That giant red blot, the image of the storm from space, looked just as menacing as the real thing.

The Psalmist David didn't need a satellite to track the thunder-storm that appears to be the immediate setting of Psalm 29. In what has become known as the 'Psalm of the Thunderstorm', he describes for us, particularly in its central section, the path of the thunderstorm—from its origin over the waters of the Mediterranean, through the north of the country, decimating the cedars of Lebanon in the process, then southwards towards the Wilderness of Kadesh, and eventually away from the Promised Land. As we journey through the psalm, it is almost as if we are watching a modern-day weather report. But then, David always managed quite well without modern technology anyway! Who can possibly read those beautiful verses of Psalm 139 without thinking of the ultrasound scans of the unborn baby that delight expectant parents as they await the birth of their child?

> For you have formed my inward parts;
> You have covered me in my mother's womb.
> I will praise you, for I am fearfully and wonderfully made;
> Marvellous are your works,
> And that my soul knows very well.
> My frame was not hidden from you,
> When I was made in secret,
> And skilfully wrought in the lowest parts of the earth.
> Your eyes saw my substance, being yet unformed.
> And in your book they were all written,
> The days fashioned for me,
> When as yet there were none of them.
>
> (Psalm 139:13-16)

So here, inspired by the Holy Spirit, and in a different way by the powerful grandeur of the thunderstorm crashing around him, David pens this glorious psalm. It is, of course, not the only composition of his that takes nature as its starting point. On the night he wrote Psalm 8, the weather must have been very different. Gazing into the heavens he exclaims:

> O LORD, our Lord,
> How excellent is your name in all the earth,
> You who set your glory above the heavens! . . .
> When I consider your heavens, the work of your fingers,
> The moon and the stars, which you have ordained,
> What is man that you are mindful of him,
> And the son of man that you visit him?
>
> (Psalm 8:1,3-4)

The weather was much better on the day he composed Psalm 19, too:

> The heavens declare the glory of God;
> And the firmament shows his handiwork . . .
> In them he has set a tabernacle for the sun,
> Which is like a bridegroom coming out of his chamber,
> And rejoices like a strong man to run its race.
> Its rising is from one end of heaven,
> And its circuit to the other end;
> And there is nothing hidden from its heat.
>
> (Psalm 19:1,4-6)

But the sun is not shining now, nor are the skies clear and starry. Yet that does not stop the Psalmist meditating upon God. If there is one thing we learn about David from reading his compositions, it is that to meditate upon God was his delight by day and night. So every time he hears the clap of thunder, he thinks about the voice of God. Indeed, the central section of the psalm reverberates with 'The voice of the LORD . . . The voice of the LORD'.

15

About this psalm, the great Charles Spurgeon wrote in his majestic commentary, *The Treasury of David*:

This [psalm] can best be rehearsed beneath the black wing of the tempest, by the glare of the lightning, or amid that dubious dusk which heralds the war of the elements. The verses march to the tune of thunderbolts.[1]

Now we know that a thunderstorm occurs when hailstones and ice, inside large cumulonimbus clouds, collide as they move up and down through the cloud. This causes particles with positive electrical charge to accumulate near the top of the cloud, and those with a negative charge to gather near the base, and then induce a positive charge on the ground below. When the charge builds beyond a certain point, it discharges as a spark of lightning. Lightning heats the air around it to up to 30,000 degrees Celsius, five times as hot as the surface of the sun, in less than a second, causing it to explode violently. Thunder is the sound of that explosion.

But, to David, the storm is much more than that! A century or more after Spurgeon preached, James Montgomery Boice wrote:

If you keep telling yourself that the voice of God is not in the thunder, that thunder is only the clashing of differently charged electronic particles, you miss it all. To appreciate this psalm we have to get out in the fields, watch the majesty of some ferocious storm, and recall that God is in the storm, directing it, as He is in all other natural and historical phenomena.[2]

The great hymn-writers of the past thought in a similar way. Listen to perhaps the prince of them all, Isaac Watts:

> The thunders of His hand
>   Keep the wide world in awe;
> His wrath and justice stand
>   To guard His holy law.[3]

16

Or the hymn of Carl Gustaf Boberg, translated by Stuart Hine:

> O Lord my God, when I in awesome wonder
> Consider all the works Thy hand hath made,
> I see the stars, I hear the mighty thunder,
> Thy power throughout the universe displayed . . .

We can learn a lot from David's use of different weather conditions to help him meditate upon his God. Christians centuries ago did so far more frequently than we do. Indeed, in bygone generations, the history books tell us, this psalm would be read to families, and even congregations, during storms. Perhaps because we have such a thorough understanding of meteorology, we have lost the wonder that our forefathers had as they watched the ever-changing elements in the sky. We can all be weather experts now!

It is a truism that when British people have nothing else to talk about they will discuss the weather, and you will not need many conversations in a day to discover someone who finds it too hot, too cold, or in some way not to their liking. But, like David, the Christian should use the weather conditions to help him meditate upon his God. Indeed, it seems reasonable to suggest, from the Scriptures, that the Creator has designed climatic conditions deliberately to help us in this activity.

Take the rain, for example. How good it would be if, instead of complaining in wet weather, God's people meditated upon Isaiah's great description of the water cycle found in that wonderful fifty-fifth chapter of his prophecy:

> For as the rain comes down, and the snow from heaven,
> And do not return there,
> But water the earth,
> And make it bring forth and bud,
> That it may give seed to the sower
> And bread to the eater,
> So shall my word be that goes forth from my mouth;

It shall not return to me void,
But it shall accomplish what I please,
And it shall prosper in the thing for which I sent it.

(Isaiah 55:10,11)

Then, instead of complaining about the wet weather, such meditation would cause the believer to pray for his pastor as, even at that moment perhaps, he will be sitting in his study preparing, and praying for, the message that God has laid on his heart—a message that will not return to God void, that will not return without bringing forth what he has desired to accomplish with it.

That verse is not the only one in Isaiah that speaks about the snow or gives us cause to meditate in wintry weather. In his first chapter, Isaiah pleads with the people of his day:

'Come now, and let us reason together,' says the Lord,
'Though your sins are like scarlet,
They shall be as white as snow;
Though they are red like crimson,
They shall be as wool.'

(Isaiah 1:18)

Perhaps Isaiah had the words of another of David's psalms in mind as he urged the people in this way. When brave Nathan the prophet had faced up to David and made David face up to his sin, David pleaded with God for forgiveness, drawing upon the picture of snow as he cried,

Purge me with hyssop, and I shall be clean;
Wash me, and I shall be whiter than snow.

(Psalm 51:7)

Why did God choose to make the snow white? And not just white, but whiter than any white the best washing powder that man will ever devise can manage? It was because he wants us to see just how white he can make our crimson, sin-laden hearts.

18

For that to happen, of course, the work of God's Spirit is needed. And if we want a picture of the Holy Spirit and his work, it is to another of the natural elements that we must turn.

One night, at the time of Passover, when the Lord Jesus Christ was in Jerusalem, an influential leader of the Jews came to him. His name was Nicodemus, and his story is told in the third chapter of John's Gospel. As Jesus explained to Nicodemus the mystery of the new birth, he drew upon the picture of the wind as he talked about the Holy Spirit. He lovingly told the ruler:

> Do not marvel that I said to you, 'You must be born again.' The wind blows where it wishes, and you hear the sound of it, but cannot tell where it comes from and where it goes. So is everyone who is born of the Spirit.
>
> (John 3:7-8)

As Nicodemus meditated that weekend on the events of the exodus from Egypt all those centuries ago, and on the deliverance through the Red Sea as God sent a mighty wind to hold back the waters and enable the people to escape on dry ground, the Saviour spoke to him of a far greater deliverance that he needed, redemption from the bondage of sin, and of a greater wind, the 'wind' of the Holy Spirit.

How God's people need to meditate upon that truth! On a windy day, O that believers would cry out for the Holy Spirit to do his work in their families, in their churches and in their land! How we need once again to hear the sound of 'a rushing mighty wind'! How we need to see the mighty work of God's Spirit devastating the lives of unbelievers with conviction of iniquity, uprooting the mighty oaks of sin in those lives, and transforming the landscapes of their rebelliousness with the righteousness of Christ!

And then, of course, there is the sun. The Psalmist thought of God himself when he meditated on the sun:

19

For the LORD God is a sun and shield;
The LORD will give grace and glory;
No good thing will he withhold
From those who walk uprightly.

(Psalm 84:11)

But, living this side of Calvary, who else could we think about, in sunny weather, but the one Malachi looked forward to, as in the last chapter of the Old Testament he strained his eyes to look over the page at what would follow?

But to you who fear my name
The Sun of Righteousness shall arise
With healing in his wings;
And you shall go out
And grow fat like stall-fed calves.

(Malachi 4:2)

Yes, just as God pointed Job to the wonders of the natural world instead of explaining to him his ways, so you and I need to use the lessons of nature to draw us nearer to God and to the Lord Jesus himself.

That was a lesson the first disciples of the Saviour learnt one night on the lake of Galilee. In the eighth chapter of his Gospel, Matthew places on record for us the busyness of the day that had preceded it. Jesus had healed a servant of a centurion of the occupying enemy. He had done so long-distance, with just a word, displaying in action the same authority that had so amazed the people as he spoke to them the great sermon that Matthew records in the three chapters immediately prior to this one.

Later that day, in Capernaum, after healing Peter's mother-in-law, the Saviour was inundated with people with sicknesses of every kind, and in his powerful, yet gentle, way, 'he cast out the spirits with a word, and healed all who were sick'. Even as he was retreating from them to the sanctuary of a boat trip across the lake, he had time and love to deal with some would-be disciples who had yet to count the cost of following the home-less Son of Man.

It is no surprise, therefore, that when he eventually reaches the boat, and the motions of the vessel on the lake begin to take their effect on his exhausted human frame, he is soon asleep. Even the sudden fierce storm, violent even for Galilee which was known for such tempests, is unable to wake the worn-out Sleeper.

The disciples, on the other hand, are rowing for their lives. The lake, with its sudden squalls, had snatched the lives of too many fishermen like them for them to underestimate the gravity of their predicament. Their faith has disappeared with the last of the stars, now hidden by the angry clouds. Whether or not there were thunder and lightning, there are certainly wind and waves, and the disciples are so busy rowing and bailing out that for a moment they have forgotten their powerful Passenger.

When the disciples eventually shake him out of his deep sleep, it is partly to reprimand him for not caring that they are perishing, but also to plead for his help. And oh, how he helps! After lovingly rebuking them for their lack of faith, he more firmly rebukes the wind and the sea: 'Peace, be still.'

The effect is as dramatic as it is instantaneous. The Gospel writers, often masters of understatement when recounting the greatest of miracles, simply tell us that there was a great calm! But if the sea of Galilee is no longer troubled, that cannot be said for the crew of this tiny fishing vessel. They marvel, saying: 'Who can this be, that even the winds and the sea obey him?'

The answer to that question is found here in Psalm 29:3.

> The voice of the LORD is over the waters;
> The God of glory thunders;
> The LORD is over many waters.

2
Angels, help us!

'Give unto the LORD, O you mighty ones,
Give unto the LORD glory and strength.'
(Psalm 29:1)

There is only one occasion every year when I am considered important enough to have a seat reserved for me. As pastor of a small fellowship in a village on the edge of the south Wales valleys, I have sought to be involved in the life of the community, and regularly have the opportunity to take the school assembly at the local infant school. Because of that, every Christmas, what I call the one 'fringe benefit' of my calling arrives on my doormat. It is an invitation to the school nativity play! And not just an invitation!

When I arrive at the school, I know that I will not need to fight my way for a seat, elbowing out of the way the assorted parents, grandparents and others who have come to see little Tommy's acting debut as the third wise man, or the back end of the donkey! Nor will I have to stand at the side of the hall, jostling for a view with dozens of proud fathers, all with their camcorders trained onto the stage so as not to miss the one line that little Jessica has been practising at home for weeks. No, for I have a reserved place in the very front row! I will have my own seat, wedged between the portly figure of my counterpart from the Methodist church, and the somewhat slimmer rector of the parish.

Nativity plays like this one take place in schools all over the country. Even in these post-Christian days of the British nation, when each and every religion competes for time in the state-school curriculum, this Christmas tradition is holding its own. Because of that, nativity plays are not normally news-worthy events.

All of that changed a couple of years ago, when one such play even made the main news bulletin of the BBC! Parents had come away from a school horrified at the way some of the essential characters of the story had been presented. The angel Gabriel, and later the angels who had sung at the appearance to the shepherds, had not been dressed in the usual way, indistinguishable from the fairy that adorns the top of many a Christmas tree! Rather they had been more like soldiers in appearance, manly, warlike—'like stormtroopers', as one visibly angry parent described it. What was the school thinking of?

A calm and thoughtful teacher, obviously the one responsible for this outrage, was interviewed. He invited those puzzled or concerned to examine the Bible, the only source material we have for what angels might look like and, more importantly, be like!

Maybe that teacher had Psalm 29, amongst other texts, in mind. Even before the thunderstorm has begun, in the first two introductory verses David has the praise of God as his focus. He calls upon the 'mighty ones' to glorify his God.

But who are these 'mighty ones'? Some commentators have argued that he is addressing the mighty men of his day; others have even suggested that he is speaking to the false gods, idols worshipped in the nations around. It seems more likely, however, that he is speaking to the angels of heaven, those celestial beings mentioned over a hundred times in the Old Testament and even more often in the New; beings that are usually invisible, exist in great numbers, and who continually worship and praise the God they serve. Allan Harman, in his recent commentary, follows in a long tradition when he concludes:

> Those addressed are most probably the angels, so that the speaker requests the angelic host to join in praise of the Lord.[4]

The Hebrew original, literally 'sons of gods', brings to our memory the opening chapter of the book of Job, and the heavenly court there. Similar language is used in another psalm:

> For who in the heavens can be compared to the LORD?
> Who among the sons of the mighty can be likened to the LORD?
>
> (Psalm 89:6)

If David is addressing the angels and encouraging them to praise their Creator, it would certainly be in keeping with several other of his psalms. Psalm 103:20, for example, which Henry Francis Lyte transformed into

> Angels, help us to adore Him;
> Ye behold Him face to face;[5]

exclaims:

> Bless the LORD, you his angels,
> Who excel in strength, who do his word,
> Heeding the voice of his word.

The same cry can be found in Psalm 148:2:

> Praise him, all his angels;
> Praise him, all his hosts!

David was not shy of addressing the angelic throng and reminding them of their duty! But why would he do that? Why tell the angels what they intended doing anyway? After all, if there is one thing that Scripture connects angels with more than anything else, it is the praise of Almighty God.

David surely recognises that he is insufficient for the praise of such a God as the One he is worshipping, and is seeking their company in the mighty work in which he is engaged. But as we continue to answer that question, we need to remind ourselves that the Psalmist is not speaking to the angels first and foremost, even though he addresses them. He is speaking to God. He is praising him! He is telling God that he is worthy of the praise of the 'mighty ones', just as Psalm 148 acknowledges him to be worthy of the praise of the whole of the created order:

> Praise him, sun and moon;
> Praise him, all you stars of light!
> Praise him, you heavens of heavens,
> And you waters above the heavens!
> (Psalm 148:3-4)

David is probably also talkng to himself as he begins this psalm of praise. That, too, is something he is never reluctant to do, as a cursory survey of the Psalter will easily show. How often have we taken ourselves by the scruff of the neck and told ourselves,

> Bless the LORD, O my soul;
> And all that is within me, bless his holy name.
> (Psalm 103:1)

Perhaps David is reminding himself of the praise of angels in order to encourage his own praise. In the small fellowship where we worship, we often feel on Sundays our numerical weakness and lack of strength. How good it is to remind ourselves that we are part of a vast company! While *we* are praising God, there are countless numbers all over the world doing the same thing. They may be in chapels, churches, cathedrals, hired halls, houses, caves or forests. They may be meeting under the vaulted ceilings of great buildings, or under palm trees on a sunny beach. But they are one with us in praising this God.

How much more encouraging it is to remember that we also add our voices to those of the angels of heaven as they sing their praise! What grand company we are keeping! That is not an original thought. It is surely part of the idea found in the epistle to the Hebrews:

But you have come to Mount Zion and to the city of the living God, the heavenly Jerusalem, to an innumerable company
of angels, to the general assembly and church of the first-born
who are registered in heaven, to God the judge of all, to the
spirits of just men made perfect.

(Hebrews 12:22-23)

Yes, the Psalmist is doing far more than telling the angels to do
what they so enjoy doing anyway.

 Not that you would think that praising God is their primary
employment, if you read much that is written about angels
nowadays! The sad truth is that in our man-centred age, almost
every aspect of the Christian faith has become man-centred too.
So when we consider angels today, our first stop tends to be the
verse where the writer asks:

Are they not all ministering spirits sent forth to minister for
those who will inherit salvation?

(Hebrews 1:14)

This first chapter of Hebrews is not actually about angels. It
focuses on the Lord Jesus Christ, and proves his supremacy over
angels with several quotes from the Old Testament. Whilst he
has 'sat', they are 'sent'. But that does not stop it being so often
the verse that grabs our attention.

 Of course, the fact that angels minister to believers is not in
doubt. It is something we rejoice in. In 2 Kings 6 we read of how
Elisha experienced it that day in Dothan, when he was surrounded by enemy chariots but, more importantly, by their heavenly superiors of fire. And, of course, the Psalmist himself tells
us,

The angel of the LORD encamps all around those who fear
 him,
And delivers them.

(Psalm 34:7)

Some of the missionary biographies of the past century or so provide us with undeniable evidence that there have been times when God's servants have owed their lives to the dramatic intervention of 'mighty ones' like those in Psalm 29. Take, for instance, the legendary John Paton, pioneer missionary to the New Hebrides. There was a night when he and his wife found themselves surrounded by cannibals. Their only weapon against those who sought their life, and whose cries they could hear nearby, was prayer. At sunrise, however, they found that the savages had retreated into the forest. Their prayers had been answered.

Months later, when the tribal chief was converted, Paton asked him about that dreadful night, and how it was that he and his wife had been spared. In reply, the chief asked Paton a question of his own:

> Who were all those men who were with you? There were hundreds of tall men in shining garments with drawn swords circling about your house, so we could not attack you![6]

Reading stories like this warms our hearts, but it sometimes makes us focus on our own lives, looking for angelic involvement. What we must never lose sight of, however, is that these ministering spirits are 'sent'—did you spot that word in Hebrews 1:14? Our focus again is directed towards God. These angels do not fly to our aid primarily because of us, or even of their own desire. They are *sent*. And responding to God's sending is part of their worship of him.

That is surely one of the lessons we can draw from Isaiah 6, one of the great passages of the Old Testament that speaks of heavenly beings. In the midst of all the political instability and uncertainty of the year of the death of an earthly monarch, Isaiah is granted a view into the throne-room of the One who is Sovereign of heaven and earth and whose kingdom is steadfast and unshakeable. There he sees an unspeakably glorious scene

of worship: seraphim circle above the throne, calling to one
another,

> Holy, holy, holy is the LORD of hosts;
> The whole earth is full of his glory!
> (Isaiah 6:3)

Even these sinless creatures recognise that they are in the presence of One who is beyond their comprehension in terms of purity
and majesty. With two of their wings, therefore, they cover their
face, unable to gaze at his awesome splendour. Their sense of
unworthiness is shown by the fact that they use two further wings
to cover their feet. O that we had such an awareness of God's
majesty and our comparative nothingness as we come to worship!

But what is equally worthy of our attention, and of our imi-
tation, is the fact that, as part of their worship of God, these
angels are continually poised to dart away at the direction of the
One upon the throne; for with their other two wings they fly.
Well did the great Richard Baxter write:

> Ye holy angels bright,
>   Who wait at God's right hand,
> Or through the realms of light
>   Fly at your Lord's command . . .

This is illustrated as Isaiah is commissioned. Even as the
prophet associates himself with the sin and the people of his
nation, one of the seraphim is sent to touch his mouth with a live
coal from the altar, and Isaiah's iniquity is purged and his sin
taken away. That the angelic beings minister to us is worthy of
our attention; but that they do so in praise and service of
Almighty God is much more important.

If ever there was a moment when to serve God was an
angel's delight, it must have been 'when the fullness of the time
had come' (Galatians 4:4). How thrilled must Gabriel have been
when he was sent to take that greatest of messages to a humble

virgin in Nazareth all those years ago! After centuries of observing the helplessness of mankind as it failed to please God, indeed of seeing us men and women in our permanent rebellion against him, how eager must the angel have been to bring good news to Mary, and to humanity in general! Is it any wonder that his first word to her is 'Rejoice!'? And then to be able to tell her of the baby that she is to bear, that he will be called Jesus—the Saviour—and that

> He will be great, and will be called the Son of the Highest; and the Lord God will give him the throne of his father David. And he will reign over the house of Jacob for ever, and of his kingdom there will be no end.
>
> (Luke 1:32-33)

Isn't this a moment, above all others, when an angel is obedient to David's command here in Psalm 29?

And what about the angel who appeared to Joseph in a dream? How incomparable is the message that he brings from the throne-room of heaven! It is that Joseph's betrothed is to

> bring forth a Son, and you shall call his name JESUS, for he will save his people from their sins.
>
> (Matthew 1:21)

Isn't this another moment, surpassing all others, when an angel is obedient to David's command here in Psalm 29? What glory and strength he ascribes to the unborn King!

And, of course, that is not the end. His birth is celebrated by a multitude of the heavenly host, who rush to earth to proclaim the newborn Messiah. They are praising God and saying,

> Glory to God in the highest,
> And on earth peace, goodwill toward men!
> (Luke 2:14)

This heavenly concert follows the good news brought to the shepherds by another angelic spokesman—news of a Saviour

who has been born, a Saviour for them, a Saviour in Bethlehem, a Saviour who is the Christ, God's anointed, a Saviour
who is Lord! Was there ever a moment when an angel was
more obedient to the exhortation of the Psalmist? Here is
ascribed such glory and strength!

But there came a time in that Saviour's life when angelic
involvement could not take place. Yes, in the Garden of
Gethsemane we do see an angel, and it is Luke who tells us
about this too. As Jesus wrestles in prayer with his Father, as he
glimpses the terror of the cup that he has to drink to the full, and
as Satan tempts him to cowardice and failure,

> Then an angel appeared to him from heaven, strengthening
> him.
>
> (Luke 22:43)

Just as he had been strengthened by ministering angels after the
victory over Satan in the wilderness, so before that great and ultimate crushing victory over the serpent at Calvary, the angels
come to his aid.

But from that moment he is on his own. Although, as he said
himself in Gethsemane, he could have called upon the Father to
provide him with more than twelve legions of angels for his personal deliverance, he does not do so. For once, the angels are
held back. He must go to Calvary alone. He must die alone, even
forsaken by his Father. He must endure the curse, for us, alone!
How wonderful is his love to us!

When death has been submitted to and gloriously defeated,
however, the angels return. Nothing can stop their praise of the
Lord now. Early that morning on the first day of the week, how
these 'mighty ones' must have rejoiced to declare the good news
of the resurrection to those crestfallen and bewildered women!

> Why do you seek the living among the dead? He is not here,
> but is risen!
>
> (Luke 24:5,6)

These 'mighty ones' are also there at the moment he ascends to his Father in heaven, and takes that seat at the right hand of the majesty on high. They will be there too when he returns to this world:

> And while they looked steadfastly toward heaven as he went up, behold, two men stood by them in white apparel, who also said, 'Men of Galilee, why do you stand gazing up into heaven? This same Jesus, who was taken up from you into heaven, will so come in like manner as you saw him go into heaven.'
>
> (Acts 1:10-11)

The 'mighty ones' who accompanied the giving of the law will accompany the return of the One who has saved us from the curse of the law, the One who kept the law in its fullness, and the One to whom, on that day, every knee will bow, and every tongue have to make confession. O that on that day we might, with surpassing joy, join with the angels as they are faithful to David's command to

> Give unto the LORD, O you mighty ones,
> Give unto the LORD glory and strength.

3
Due glory

'Give unto the LORD, O you mighty ones,
Give unto the LORD glory and strength.
Give unto the LORD the glory due to his name.'
(Psalm 29:1-2a)

Anyone growing up, as I did, in 1970s Britain, soon became familiar with the idea of a 'differential'. That decade was one of the worst in British history in terms of industrial relations. Millions of days were lost to strike action, and successive governments were held to ransom by trade union leaders, who carried with them into their pay negotiations the realistic threat of paralysing the country. And the key word was often 'differentials'.

Everybody had an idea of what the right wage for their job ought to be. Everybody had an idea of how their vocation compared with that of the man who lived next door, or who stood next to them in the bus queue on the way to work in the morning. If he had had a pay rise, they must be due one too. And if someone they judged to be below them in the order of things overtook them, well, that was just too much. The result, of course, was a circular succession of strikes in key industries, as everybody sought to protect their rung on the payscales of British society.

In the decades that have followed, the increased competition for jobs in a global market has, perhaps, forced a more realistic view in that area of life. But men and women still fight to establish their rights in other spheres. Indeed a veritable 'rights' industry has been spawned, with legal advisers making a mint out of such an attitude. A burglar caught in the act on the premises of a householder, will go to court if he feels he has been manhandled too roughly by the occupant defending his property. The child excluded from a succession of schools, due to her bad behaviour, takes the local authority to court to establish her 'right' to be provided with an education. On a more emotionally difficult level, we hear and sympathise with the cry of a childless couple who plead their rights to be provided with repeated courses of an expensive medical procedure, which is their only hope of a family.

The claim for human rights has never been louder. The irony is, of course, that it comes from a society where people are less and less willing to face up to their responsibilities as members of such a society. As the members of any group of people, even a golf club or a local church, know, there can be no rights without responsibilities.

It is important to remember that the first and most groundbreaking book ever to be written establishing 'human rights' was, of course, the Bible. In Old Testament times, Almighty God delighted to be known as the protector of the fatherless and the widow, and the levitical law of the early pages of God's Word is saturated with detailed provisions establishing the 'rights' to be accorded to the most vulnerable in society. They were the most paradoxical of concepts—rights flowing exclusively from the grace of God!

The New Testament is equally radical in its own way. Those who call the apostle Paul a male chauvinist, as even bishops of the Anglican church are often heard to do, only reveal the depths of their ignorance. In terms of the society in which Paul was writing, the 'rights' that he gave women within a marriage relationship, particularly in 1 Corinthians, were off the scale.

Divine rights

But in the first verses of Psalm 29, it is not human rights that are in view, but divine rights. As David calls upon the 'mighty ones', he reminds them of what rightly belongs to God. He calls upon them in verse 2 to

Give unto the LORD the glory due to his name.

Here is a very helpful place to start our study of this verse. God is worthy of worship. He deserves our honour and praise. When we come before God, we are not doing him a favour. Indeed, the privilege of worshipping such a mighty God is all ours. That he should ever condescend to accept the praise of angels, beings that he has created, even though they are sinless, is grace indeed. That he should ever find a way of accepting the worship of sinful wretches like us should take our breath away!

The other side of the coin rolling from that thought is that when we deny God our praise and worship, we are doing just that: we are denying him what is rightly his; we are not giving him his rights. When we refuse to set aside time each day for him, framing as an excuse the busyness of our lives, we are not giving God his rights. When we get out of bed on a Lord's Day, and ponder whether we will bother to attend public worship once, let alone twice, we are robbing God of what is rightfully his. When areas of our lives are effectively roped off from the lordship of Christ, we are being disobedient to the command that this verse evidently lays upon us. No, there are no rights without responsibilities. Our responsibility is to give him his rights!

This psalm, indeed this verse, helps us in a more detailed way, however. For it reminds us not only of our responsibility to praise God, but also of how we are to do it. How am I to approach God? How am I to worship him?

To begin to answer that question, it is worth pondering a few other words that appear in the first half of verse 2. Take the word 'Give', right at its beginning, and indeed at the beginning of both parts of the first verse also. The Hebrew word in the original is probably better translated 'ascribe'. That is the way it has been translated in another Bible verse, one that has been helpfully set to music in recent years:

> Ascribe greatness to our God.
> He is the Rock, his work is perfect;
> For all his ways are justice,
> A God of truth and without injustice;
> Righteous and upright is he.
> (Deuteronomy 32:3b,4)

The idea of ascribing something to God, both here and in that verse from the Song of Moses, surely carries an overpowering thought with it. Our worship of God should be thoughtful and considered. Before we can ascribe something to somebody, we have to pause and think about it.

Maybe you have agreed to act as a referee for someone applying for a job. Back has come a letter from the potential employer, asking you for a description of the applicant. How would you go about answering it? You do not hurriedly write the first thing that comes to you, but you meditate and consider what is truthful about this person's character, and only then do you begin your description, indeed your ascription. By using this Hebrew word, David encourages the 'mighty ones', and us, to do just that with Almighty God. When we approach him, we begin with his *character*.

That is underlined by the last verse of the section we are looking at for the moment. We are to give God the glory due to his 'name'. Surely the same truth is being emphasised here. When the Bible uses the word 'name', it is, of course, talking about more than the label attached to a person, or the word we use to gain that person's attention.

In Scripture, 'name' is intimately connected with character. Some Bible characters reflected their names, many because they were given names, prophetically perhaps, by their parents. Others had their names changed by God to names that would more perfectly reflect his plan and purpose for their lives. The same is true when we consider God. When David spoke of God's name, he thought of all that that name represented. He approached God on the basis of what he knew of his character, and found ample substance for his praise there.

This, of course, is the biblical way. We have already seen how Moses did just that in Deuteronomy 32. Look at the prayer of Nehemiah, voiced amidst his heartbreak at the state of Jerusalem. How does he start? Not with his needs, but with God's character:

> LORD God of heaven, O great and awesome God, you who keep your covenant and mercy with those who love you and observe your commandments . . .
>
> (Nehemiah 1:5)

This is an important issue in the man-centred age in which the church lives, and by which she is so often infected. Judging by the way he is approached by some, God has become little more than a juke box to which we saunter with our request, and whom we then expect to deliver. To others, God is just the first-aid box to which we turn in times of crisis.

Public worship often shows little of the thought and meditation that a verse like this calls from us. How many university Christian Unions are populated by intelligent young people, who spend the whole of the rest of the week engaging their minds with the great issues of 'life, the universe and everything', but who will only give the speaker at their meetings ten minutes to bring God's Word to them! Their mind has been left in the lecture room or laboratory.

The reason that churches have become involved in what is known as 'worship wars' is surely related to this too. Some have advocated changing public worship altogether. 'People from outside', they say, 'are not going to cross the threshold of our church buildings, unless what they find inside is attractive to their twenty-first-century tastes! The church is in a crowded market-place for the time and attention of people, and so we must compete with the world outside! Anything that they won't understand, or that they feel uncomfortable with, must go. The user-friendly church is what we need!'

On the other side are those who say a resounding no to such thinking. 'The church exists for the people within it, not those outside. *We* decide what we like; we have already decided, in fact, and we are not going to change. We have always worshipped like this, with this pattern of worship, and we are not going to alter anything!'

Both of these types of thinking miss the point. We worship God on the basis of who he is. He sets the terms. He appoints the way. He defines the methods. When we forget that, the church has lost true worship, whatever we replace it with.

That must be particularly true when we see exactly what it is that we are to ascribe to God. Glory! Glory and strength! Strength is something that is ascribed to God in other psalms of David:

> Ascribe strength to God;
> His excellence is over Israel,
> And his strength is in the clouds.
> (Psalm 68:34)

> O Lord God of hosts,
> Who is mighty like you, O Lord?
> Your faithfulness also surrounds you . . .
> You have a mighty arm;
> Strong is your hand.
> (Psalm 89:8,13)

Glory is one of the threads that runs right the way through this psalm. As the storm begins in verse 3, God is the God of glory, who thunders. Meanwhile, as the storm dies down in verse 9, everyone in his temple says, 'Glory!'

Glory is a theme that runs through the Psalter as a whole. A glance at a concordance shows that the word is used over forty times throughout the book, as well as in further verses where God is described as 'glorious'. 'Glory' is also used in some of the most famous verses in the Psalms.

In an earlier study we saw how, as David surveyed nature, he exclaimed: 'The heavens declare the glory of God'. In Psalm 72, another psalmist exclaims:

> Blessed be the LORD God, the God of Israel,
> Who only does wondrous things!
> And blessed be his glorious name for ever!
> And let the whole earth be filled with his glory.
> Amen and Amen.
>
> (Psalm 72:18-19)

Anybody who thought that worldwide mission is only a theme of the New Testament has not read that verse, or David's command in Psalm 96:

> Declare his glory among the nations,
> His wonders among all peoples.
>
> (Psalm 96:3)

Indeed, his glory must be declared because he is the King of glory, as Psalm 24 repeatedly declares:

> Who is this King of glory?
> The LORD strong and mighty,
> The LORD mighty in battle . . .
> The LORD of hosts,
> He is the King of glory.
>
> (Psalm 24:8,10)

But what is 'glory'? Hardly a Sunday goes by in any church without the singing of at least one hymn that uses the word, but many of those singers could no more define it than they could explain the workings of a nuclear reactor. What is this glory that we are to ascribe to the Lord?

The truth is that it is not an easy word to describe. It seems to be made up of a number of ideas. Its root idea is that of 'heaviness', 'weightiness', 'substance', but included in it are other ideas such as honour, light, splendour and majesty. All these things belong to God.

As a child, one of the treats that I remember on a visit to the seaside was the candyfloss sold, perhaps, at the shop at the end of the pier. Deliciously sticky, melting in your mouth, it was a fun way to end a fun day. But the trouble with candyfloss is that once you've taken a mouthful, it's gone! It has no substance, no reality, and certainly no goodness.

The so-called real world that we inhabit is actually a 'candyfloss' world. Its pleasures are like candyfloss, fun to the senses, attractive to the taste-buds, but of no value at all. They leave us with nothing more permanent than tooth decay, a burgeoning waistline, and a vaguely sick feeling.

How good it is to be able to focus on Someone with substance, Someone with a 'weightiness' beyond anything the world can offer. What is more, this glorious God is light and majesty, and full of splendour!

It is the apostle Paul who tells us something most important about the glory of God:

For it is the God who commanded light to shine out of darkness who has shone in our hearts to give the light of the knowledge of the glory of God in the face of Jesus Christ.

(2 Corinthians 4:6)

We know something of the glory of God when we gaze upon the Lord Jesus Christ. As John tells us in the beginning of his Gospel:

And the Word became flesh and dwelt among us, and we beheld his glory, the glory as of the only begotten of the Father, full of grace and truth.

(John 1:14)

There were times in his earthly ministry when that glory was most openly displayed. On the Mount of Transfiguration, the Moses who had had a previous mountain-top experience of the glory of God on Sinai, and the Elijah who had revisited the same spot for a similar purpose centuries later, came face to face with that glory.

The miracles of Jesus, too, displayed something of his glory. John again tells us this after the Saviour's first miracle, the changing of the water into wine, portraying the inauguration of the gospel age:

> This beginning of signs Jesus did in Cana of Galilee, and manifested his glory.
>
> (John 2:11)

But when the use of the word 'glory' is traced through the fourth Gospel, it can be seen that it is the hour of dedication to death which is the hour of glory. As Judas leaves the upper room, the Saviour says:

> Now the Son of Man is glorified, and God is glorified in him.
>
> (John 13:31)

As he faces what is outwardly the most inglorious moment in his life here on earth, he begins his high-priestly prayer to the Father with the cry:

> And now, O Father, glorify me together with yourself, with the glory which I had with you before the world was.
>
> (John 17:5)

In the hours that he hung, bearing our sin, upon the cross at Calvary, there was no one to ascribe unto the Lord glory and strength. There seemed to be no glory in such weakness. But, as the apostle Paul reminded the church at Philippi, it was because of what happened on that hill outside the city wall, that there will come a day when the whole world will give him the glory due to his name:

> And being found in appearance as a man, he humbled himself and became obedient to the point of death, even the death of the cross. Therefore God also has highly exalted him and given him the name which is above every other name, that at the name of Jesus every knee should bow, of those in heaven, and of those on earth, and of those under the earth, and that every tongue should confess that Jesus Christ is Lord, to the glory of God the Father.
>
> (Philippians 2:8-11)

On that day, everything will be different. No knee will remain unbent, no tongue will remain silent, for all will

> Give unto the LORD the glory due to his name.

4
Beautiful worship

'Worship the Lord in the beauty of holiness.'
(Psalm 29:2b)

It had been built in the aftermath of the Welsh revival of 1859. Colliery workers had given their spare pennies towards its construction, and the most gifted amateurs from the congregation had given up all their spare time to erect their 'Bethel'. Faded sepia photographs still exist that record the day that the building opened. According to local legend, the great Spurgeon preached there once, and in the times of the 1904 revival even the balcony was packed, as people filled every spare seat to be part of the services.

But then decline had set in. The theological liberalism that had infected the training colleges at the end of the nineteenth century began to spread to the denominations in the first decades of the twentieth, and inevitably trickled down to the churches a short time later. Shorn of men by two world wars, and by a great depression that sent many out of the valley in search of work elsewhere, those churches were struggling. Turning to using the building for concerts and singing festivals had provided a short-term boost, but had proved a long-term disaster. The congregation declined even faster than the industry of the town around it. The prayer meeting disappeared first, then the Sunday school, and now all that was left was one Sunday service and the mid-week ladies meeting.

It was after one of those Wednesday gatherings that somebody smelt it first. The man from the council was sent for, and he gave the disastrous news. There was dry rot in the pulpit and it was spreading to the pews. It was too far gone! And so the fateful day arrived, and with it came the bulldozers. By the time the longest-standing member had arrived to pay a fond farewell, the front walls of the chapel were already down and the side walls were crumbling. Still visible through the dust cloud, and still standing, was the back wall, displaying the elegantly scrolled text upon which the worshippers had gazed every Sunday:

O worship the LORD in the beauty of holiness.

(Psalm 29:2b, AV)

At a time when it has been estimated that one chapel building closes every week in Wales, it is not stretching the imagination too far to describe such a scenario. Whilst many buildings close, other churches, as already indicated, are trying all kinds of things as part of their services, to attract new people in, keep their buildings open and their history alive. And in many of these buildings, from high on the chapel wall the same verse stares down accusingly at their efforts: 'O worship the LORD in the beauty of holiness.'

Though David is continuing to speak first and foremost to the 'mighty ones', as he does throughout these first two verses, he is also speaking to himself and to us, who are reading God's Word three thousand years later. There are, perhaps, few verses in the whole of the Psalter that have more to say to us today than this one.

For this verse speaks of *worship*. Though all that we said in the last chapter was also about worship, it is here that the word appears for the first time. It is not the first time for it to appear in the book, of course. It is possible to make the case that the worship of God is the main theme of this longest book of the Bible. Listen to Geoffrey Grogan:

When most people think of the Book of Psalms, they view it as a worship manual . . . Not only have the psalms been used as chants and in metrical form, but many hymns and modern Christian songs show their influence.

The psalms are not only relevant to worship but of great value for this purpose in every age and place. The marvellous presupposition of this is that God seeks fellowship with His people, that He has made provision for this, and that, in the psalms, there is material for worship and for use in personal prayer.[7]

Although the Scriptures use a wide vocabulary when they talk of worship, in both Old and New Testaments, there are probably two themes that are paramount. The one is 'service', using vocabulary drawn from the world of slaves and hired servants. The other is that of 'bowing down'. When we put those ideas together, it can be clearly seen that if we are to offer God acceptable service, we are to bow down before him.

 This idea can be seen in some of the other places where David speaks about worship:

> Oh come, let us worship and bow down;
> Let us kneel before the LORD our Maker.
> For he is our God . . .
>
> (Psalm 95:6,7)

Or, a few psalms later:

> Exalt the LORD our God,
> And worship at his footstool;
> For he is holy.
>
> (Psalm 99:5)

We are immediately brought face-to-face with the challenge, therefore, that everything that we do in public worship must be in humble subservience to the fact that God is God. If we expand our thinking in line with the biblical definition of worship being the service of God, that must be true of every area of our lives.

 Let's think first about when we gather together as God's people. It is clear that recognising God as God will have a great impact on the spirit in which we approach him, and on the activities in which we will engage as we do so. Though David had, perhaps, only the Books of Moses as God's Word, they are replete with instruction on this issue, leaving him in little doubt that God could not be approached in a casual manner. They also provide us with evidence of how God feels when that guidance is slighted, and man chooses to approach him in his own way. Whenever we introduce something new or different into the public worship of God's people, we need to be absolutely sure that the Scriptures give us permission to do so. If we do anything else, however good our intention, we are not on bended knee but standing proudly in our own understanding; not recognising God as God but making ourselves God; and so we are not truly worshipping.

Every area of our lives must be offered to this God. He is God, and demands that we recognise him as such. Our work, our leisure activities, our family life and our personal life must flow from a bowed head and a bent knee. It is a recognition that we are servants of his that should control our actions and our thought processes. As Derek Kidner has pointed out in his commentary on this verse, if the first part of the verse has encouraged us to use our minds to think about the God that we are approaching, the second part enlists our wills to take the humble attitude of the servant.[8]

The verse continues in several ways that help us in the question of submitting to God and worshipping him as he is. How wonderful it is that we are to worship not just the Lord, but the LORD! We have, perhaps, been a little remiss in getting this far into the psalm without recognising the capitalisation of this title, a feature that occurs wherever his name is mentioned in Psalm 29 (which is in every verse except one). He has already been called 'the LORD' twice in verse 1, and again in the first half of this verse.

In many English versions of the Old Testament, in about three-quarters of the instances when the word 'Lord' occurs, it is spelt with capitals in this way. This is to distinguish between times when the original is talking about God in terms of him being simply 'lord' or 'master', and times when the sacred, proper name of God—the name that the Israelites thought was too holy even to utter—was being used.

When we consider this issue, the passage from Exodus 3 immediately springs to mind. There, God commissions Moses as the deliverer who will lead his people out of Egypt and to the border of the Promised Land. In this passage God lays great stress on his name and on its meaning.

Initially God introduces himself as God (*elohim*), the God of his forefathers. But Moses wants more than that. He asks God:

> Indeed, when I come to the children of Israel, and say to them, 'The God of your fathers has sent me to you', and they say to me, 'What is his name?' what shall I say to them?
>
> (Exodus 3:13)

Moses is asking for a revelation of God's nature that will authenticate him as having been sent by the true God. Maybe he also wanted more evidence to present to the Israelites that this God was able to deliver them from their horrendous predicament. The answer that Moses received did both of these things:

> And God said to Moses, 'I AM WHO I AM.' And he said, 'Thus you shall say to the children of Israel, "I AM has sent me to you."'
>
> (Exodus 3:14)

Although the commentators and the Hebrew experts argue long and hard about the exact meaning of those words, it seems clear that they are referring to God as the One who is, and who always will be, One who is dynamic and active, reliable and consistent.

The next verse goes on to identify the fact that this God is the LORD God of Moses' fathers, the God of Abraham, Isaac and Jacob, and that this will be his name for ever. The God that

Moses and the people were to worship is the God the patriarchs worshipped. He is the self-sufficient, self-revealing, active, covenant-keeping God. It is to this 'LORD' that David repeatedly turns our attention in this and many of his other psalms.

So, returning to our verse, the God that we are to bow down before and to serve is not just a changeless, active, almighty God, but One who has chosen to reveal himself to his people and to enter into a covenant with them. We are not just to worship 'God', but to worship 'the LORD'!

For the 'mighty ones' that the Psalmist is addressing that might seem an easy thing. They are there in his presence. They are not living here amidst the ugliness of a sin-ravaged world, but in the splendour and beauty of the holy dwelling place of a holy God. As we have seen in an earlier chapter, they meditate upon his holiness as they serve him, and call to one another in his praise.

But here upon earth, David encourages us to seek to do the same. We do not worship, whether with our lips or our lives, a remote, disinterested God, with whom we can have no relation-ship, and hence no reality in our worship. The God we come before, and live before, has committed himself to us. He has made promises to us, and he has been faithful in keeping those promises. He wants us to approach him on the basis of who he is and what he has done for us, and what he has promised us, particularly in the person of his Son, Jesus Christ.

That is why we need to know our God. Not just know him, but really know him! He should be our meditation day and night. He should be our delight. The more of him that we know, the richer will be our Christian lives, and the brighter will be our witness in the godless world in which he has called us to live.

How much have you grown in your knowledge of God over, say, the last year? When was the last time you read a book about God, his attributes, his character? There is nothing wrong with reading books about mission work, or biographies even of great

Christians. They have a place in encouraging us in our personal walk with the Lord, and in helping us to see our place in the worldwide church of God. But once in a while we should read something about God himself. And when that drives us to the Scriptures, as it inevitably will, we should be searching for God in them especially.

As we seek to get to know this LORD that we are to worship, we will not travel far along the road before we come across his holiness. Again, this is a theme that David returns to throughout the Psalter:

> But you are holy,
> Who inhabit the praises of Israel.
> > (Psalm 22:3)

> God reigns over the nations;
> God sits on his holy throne.
> > (Psalm 47:8)

> He has sent redemption to his people;
> He has commanded his covenant for ever:
> Holy and awesome is his name.
> > (Psalm 111:9)

Throughout the Bible, holiness, whether it speaks of God, or of people, or even of things, carries with it the idea of separation from sin, being set apart, having a quality of 'otherness'. In this verse the mighty ones, and through it God's people, are encouraged to

> Worship the LORD in the beauty of holiness.

It is not immediately clear whether the holiness that is being referred to is that of the creatures themselves, or the atmosphere of the heavenly realm, or indeed of God himself. But it seems that, just as the first part of the verse has encouraged us to meditate upon his *character*, as we bring him the glory that is due to his name, so in the second half of the verse we are being pointed to his chief characteristic.

What is more, that holiness has a *beauty*, a splendour. The Hebrew word for beauty is a completely different one from that which is used elsewhere in the Scripture to denote human attractiveness. Its root word is used elsewhere in the Psalms to denote honour or splendour. David says:

> I will meditate on the glorious splendour of your majesty,
> And on your wondrous works.
>
> (Psalm 145:5)

In the eighth psalm this same word is used to describe man:

> For you have made him a little lower than the angels,
> And you have crowned him with glory and honour.
>
> (Psalm 8:5)

The writer to the Hebrews tells us that this verse speaks ultimately about the Lord Jesus Christ, and goes on to tell us:

> But we see Jesus, who was made a little lower than the angels, for the suffering of death crowned with glory and honour, that he, by the grace of God, might taste death for everyone.
>
> (Hebrews 2:9)

When we think about it, the whole of this verse in Psalm 29 is speaking of Christ too. The New Testament writers were never afraid to take verses in the Old Testament that talked about the LORD and apply them to the Lord Jesus Christ. They had come to see that he was the One in whom all the fullness of the covenant-keeping God dwelt bodily. We see, too, displayed throughout his life a perfect and a beautiful, splendid holiness. He was able to look people in the eye, and challenge them to point a finger at any area of his life and convince him of sin. They could not do it, because though he was tried and tested in every point like us, he was without sin.

That holiness was testified to in his life by demons, and at his death by a criminal. Luke tells us of the day in Capernaum when a man with an unclean spirit was found in the synagogue. At the sight of Jesus, we are told, he cried out:

> Let us alone! What have we to do with you, Jesus of Nazareth? Did you come to destroy us? I know you, who you are —the Holy One of God!
>
> (Luke 4:34)

At the end of his life he was put to death, convicted of trumped-up charges, and vindicated by a dying thief, who knew that the Man on the cross next to him had done nothing amiss.

The wonder of that death on the cross is that the righteousness of this Holy One can be applied to us. Paul says:

> For he made him who knew no sin to be made sin for us, that we might become the righteousness of God in him.
>
> (2 Corinthians 5:21)

In 1875, there was a church building in Guildford, near London, that needed a great deal of restoration work. Thankfully, it could be saved from the nineteenth-century equivalent of the bulldozer. Sadly, however, whilst the work was being undertaken, a piece of masonry fell from the roof, striking the church's rector on the head and causing him a fatal injury. His name was John Samuel Bewley Monsell, and when he died, not only did his church lose their under-shepherd, but the church as a whole a fine hymn-writer.

Monsell's best-known hymn is undoubtedly, 'Fight the good fight', but a close second might be one that he had penned some fifteen years before his death. Its first and last verses read:

> O worship the Lord in the beauty of holiness;
> Bow down before Him, His glory proclaim;
> With gold of obedience and incense of lowliness,
> Kneel and adore Him; the Lord is His name.

Because the One who is the LORD has left the beauty and splendour of the holiness of heaven and come to this unholy world, and because this Holy One has shed his blood on Calvary, we can be clothed in his righteousness. We are also empowered to fight that good fight, until the day that we are summoned to the place where we will join with the 'mighty ones' and hear heaven's thunder, as the apostle John did:

> Then I looked, and behold, a Lamb standing on Mount Zion, and with him one hundred and forty-four thousand, having his Father's name written on their foreheads. And I heard a voice from heaven, like the voice of many waters, and like the voice of loud thunder. And I heard the sound of harpists playing their harps. And they sang as it were a new song . . .
>
> (Revelation 14:1-3)

And there we shall for ever

Worship the LORD in the beauty of holiness.

5
Powerful and majestic

'The voice of the LORD is powerful;
The voice of the LORD is full of majesty.'
(Psalm 29:4)

I have a colleague who ministers in a small church on the out-skirts of London. Every Sunday evening the service used to start in the same way. The worship would be committed to the Lord in prayer, and the number of the first hymn announced. But although God's praise then sung by the fellowship was no doubt heard in heaven, what was happening overhead meant that it could not be heard on earth. The church building, you see, is about two miles from London Heathrow Airport, and before it was decommissioned, Concorde used to take off at 6 p.m. each Sunday evening for its flight to the United States. As the con-gregation raised their voices against the background noise, the pastor told me, he would pray that when he came to preach he might enjoy the same degree of power.

Aeroplanes are just one of the loudest things in the very noisy world in which we live. Whether it is traffic, machinery, crowds at sporting occasions, or even just the general hubbub of life, we all often long for a little peace and quiet. Often a peal of thunder will go unheard against everything else that is happen-ing in our busy cities.

It is, therefore, hard for us to relate to the world that David inhabited. Almost certainly, a clap of thunder was the loudest noise he ever heard. Even when we bear in mind the military nature of much of his life, the loudest sound he would ever have heard on the battlefield would have been the clash of sword on shield. Nowadays, we measure noise in decibels. An overhead thunderstorm may reach 120 decibels, louder even than someone yelling in your ear, which has been measured at 114 decibels. The average human conversation will only be just over halfway along that scale. The only things you and I are likely to hear that are louder, particularly if we never sit in the front row at a rock concert (150 decibels), might be a nearby pneumatic drill, jet engine, or police siren. David had no experience of any of these things. Indeed, in nature, the only noises that are louder are the call of the blue whale (188 decibels) and a volcano. So we can safely say that David never heard a louder sound than he did on the day that he watched this storm.

And so, as he meditated upon God whilst transfixed by the thunder and lightning, it was natural for a godly man like him to think about Jehovah and the power of his voice. Knowing his Old Testament history, I suspect he thought of the occasion when God's voice was heard as powerfully as ever, again against the backdrop of thunder and lightning.

The people of Israel had left Egypt that first Passover night, and then experienced the miraculous deliverance at the Red Sea. The noise of thundering hooves, as Pharoah's army sought to follow God's people on the dry pathway through the flood, had been replaced by the anguished yells of drowning soldiers. That event too, according to Psalm 77:16-20, had been accompanied by thunder and earthquake. God had called his people out of Egypt that they might worship him. They had already experienced God's deliverance and his miraculous provision, but now they were going to see God's power and his holiness.

In the third month after leaving the land of bondage, they reached Sinai. There the Lord called Moses to meet with him on the mountain, a mountain that became so permeated by God's holiness that any animal that strayed on to it had to be killed— and not just killed, but killed from a safe distance. Not a human hand could touch the beast. There the Lord came down upon Mount Sinai in the sight of all the people. Exodus 19 records for us the event in its fullness, played out against the background of thunderings and lightnings. Exodus 20 summarises the law that the God of holiness proclaimed to Moses. The verses immediately following the Decalogue tell us:

> Now all the people witnessed the thunderings, the lightning flashes, the sound of the trumpet, and the mountain smoking; and when the people saw it, they trembled and stood afar off. Then they said to Moses, 'You speak with us and we will hear; but let not God speak with us, lest we die.'
>
> (Exodus 20:18-19)

Deuteronomy 18 tells us of the long-term result of the terrified plea of the people. In words that the apostle Peter, in Solomon's Portico, said had their ultimate fulfilment in the Lord Jesus Christ, God made the people a promise, which Moses repeated to them:

> The LORD your God will raise up for you a Prophet like me from your midst, from your brethren. Him you shall hear, according to all you desired of the LORD your God in Horeb, in the day of the assembly, saying, 'Let me not hear again the voice of the LORD my God, nor let me see this great fire any more, lest I die.'
>
> (Deuteronomy 18:15-16)

Why did the people fear hearing the voice of the Lord? David has the answer:

> The voice of the LORD is powerful;
> The voice of the LORD is full of majesty.

Sinai, of course, was not the first occasion when God's voice had caused such dramatic effects! The Bible opens with perhaps the greatest display of God's power seen until the day of the resurrection of the Saviour. And everything that God did on the six days of creation, until he took the dust of the earth to form man, he did simply with his voice.

On the day that God began to make the world, there was no noise. The only sound that was deafening was the silence. For 'the earth was without form and void'. There was certainly no thunder, but neither was there the sound of birds singing, trees swaying, insects buzzing, animals moving, or people communicating. There was no sound because there was no thing. Then suddenly a voice, powerful and majestic, broke through the stillness that had lasted throughout eternity: 'Let there be light.' The first sound ever to be heard was the voice of Almighty God himself. Only there was nobody and nothing to hear it. An audience for his words would not be called into existence until a few days later.

The response to the voice was immediate and dramatic. Genesis simply records, 'and there was light'. There is no explanation as to how, or why, or when; just the record of the instantaneous response to the summons of God. It is left to David to give us the explanation:

> The voice of the LORD is powerful;
> The voice of the LORD is full of majesty.

And this was no isolated event. On day two of the week of creation, the same powerful, majestic voice decrees the placing of the firmament between the waters above and below it. And it was so. We hear him again on day three, gathering the waters under the heaven together, calling dry land into existence, and causing it to bring forth grass and herbs and trees. And it was so. During the next three days, by the same word of power and majesty, God sets about filling the universe he has made. Lights in the heavens, which, as we have already seen, lead David to praise God in others of his psalms, are called into being on day four; abundant living creatures to fill the seas and skies on day five, and animals to fill the earth on day six. Now the world truly is a noisy place—and not just a place of sounds, but also of colours and smells, tastes and textures. Every one of our senses can enjoy God's world, because the sixth day of creation culminates with the apex of God's handiwork, as the same powerful and majestic voice declares:

Let us make man in our image, according to our likeness . . .
(Genesis 1:26)

After every act of creation, we are left in no doubt as to the effectiveness of the voice, and of the One from whom it comes. We are simply and emphatically told, 'and it was so'. Neither are we to question the quality of what has been produced, for the chorus resounds throughout the chapter: 'And God saw that it was good.' How right David was in this verse:

The voice of the LORD is powerful;
The voice of the LORD is full of majesty.

No, Sinai was not the first occasion when God's voice was heard. Neither would it be the last! It was heard again thousands of years later, when the Word, the Word made flesh that dwelt amongst us, walked upon the planet that he had so effortlessly created.

At the commencement of his ministry, he went to the river Jordan, where John was baptising. There Jesus too was baptised, and as he came up out of the water, Mark tells us:

He saw the heavens parting and the Spirit descending upon him like a dove. Then a voice came from heaven, 'You are my beloved Son, in whom I am well pleased.'
(Mark 1:10b-11)

The Gospel writers tell us of two other occasions when the voice of God sounded from the heavens. Matthew, Mark and Luke tell us of the day the Saviour took Peter, James and John up a high mountain by themselves. They were soon joined by two great figures from history, two men who had had mountain-top experiences with God before, Moses and Elijah. Before their faces the Lord Jesus was transfigured:

> His clothes became shining, exceedingly white, like snow, such as no launderer on earth can whiten them.
>
> (Mark 9:3)

And Mark records in verse 7 that the same voice as was heard at the baptism called out with the same acclamation:

> This is my beloved Son, hear him!

Though John does not record the transfiguration in his Gospel, he tells us about another occasion, one which has a peculiar connection with the verse we are looking at from Psalm 29. Just days before Passover, Jesus had ridden into Jerusalem, to the sound of children shouting 'Hosanna'. The city was busy, with pilgrims from all over the known world. Some Greeks had come to Philip telling him of their desire to see Jesus. The message was relayed to the Master, who, in turn, proclaims that the hour, the hour that the whole of John's Gospel has anticipated, has come. The answer that the Lord gives to Philip soon turns into a prayer, a prayer that the Father would glorify his name. At that point, John tells us:

> Then a voice came from heaven, saying, 'I have both glorified it and will glorify it again.'
>
> (John 12:28)

Everybody heard the voice, the apostle writes, but very few believed that the voice had a divine origin. Instead thay assumed that it was thunder! How ironic, that whereas David heard the thunder and thought of the voice of God, those who rejoiced in their Davidic heritage heard the voice of God and thought it was thunder! How right it is, when the Bible says that only those who have ears to hear, will hear!

Do I have ears to hear? Do I come to the Scriptures listening for the voice of Almighty God to speak to me through the sacred pages of his Word? That Word is the book that tells me about God the Son, who is the fulfilment of this verse in David's psalm.

Did ever the voice of God sound upon earth with more power and majesty than when the Saviour walked amongst men? We have already thought of his power to still the storm on the lake, and to do so with just a word. But what about some of those other occasions?

What about that occasion recorded in Mark 7, when Jesus healed a deaf man in the region of Decapolis around Galilee? That man's world had been silent, as silent as the world was in the moments before God created. He is brought to Jesus by friends who beg that the divine Physician would put his hands upon him. Jesus graciously takes him to one side, away from the prying gaze of the nosey onlookers, people who had probably stared at the man throughout his life. Jesus places his fingers in the man's ears, puts spittle on the man's lips, and looks to heaven with a sigh. He then utters the last word that the man would fail to hear—*Ephphatha*! And they were opened! From now on his hearing would be one hundred per cent. The first voice he had heard was the Saviour's, the voice that David had described a millennium before:

> The voice of the LORD is powerful;
> The voice of the LORD is full of majesty.

That powerful, majestic voice was able to give the blind their sight, make the lame to walk, and to call demons, even legions of them, out of possessed men. That voice was even able to raise the dead. In the house of a ruler of a synogogue he utters the words '*Talitha cumi*' and a twelve-year-old girl is restored to life. On a track on the outskirts of Nain, a boy about to be buried by his widowed mother responds to the summons, 'Young man, I say to you, arise!' At a graveside outside the village of

Bethany, two weeping sisters mourn their dead brother, until he calls, 'Lazarus, come forth.' Four days after his death, Lazarus is more alive than ever! Such is the power, such is the majesty of the voice of the incarnate God!

How wonderful that that same Lord, the One in whom all the fullness of the Godhead dwelt bodily, used that same powerful, majestic voice to call people to himself! Moreover, he still does! The voice that summoned Lazarus from physical death, on the same occasion said:

I am the Resurrection and the Life. He who believes in me, though he may die, he shall live. And whoever lives and believes in me shall never die.

(John 11:25-26)

And the same voice of power and majesty graciously said:

Come to me, all who labour and are heavy laden, and I will give you rest. Take my yoke upon you and learn from me, for I am gentle and lowly in heart, and you will find rest for your souls. For my yoke is easy and my burden is light.

(Matthew 11:28-29)

I imagine that such words were said quietly and compassionately, as well as powerfully and majestically. For true power and majesty does not need to shout. To raise Lazarus from the grave he had used a 'loud voice', but that was a rare occurrence. Elsewhere in the Gospels we hear of demons crying with a loud voice, and others in need of physical healing doing likewise. We read of people praising God, and thanking the Saviour with a loud voice. But the only loud speaking the Son of Man does, is by his actions.

There was only one other occasion that the Gospel writers choose to tell us about when the Saviour used a 'loud voice'. It was, possibly, when his power and majesty were, at the same time, both the most hidden and the most openly declared!

59

The loud voices that had filled the air that night had not been singing their hosannas. They had been crying 'Crucify him! Crucify him!' The spotless Lamb of God had been taken from judgement, and led out of the city to be crucified. At the Place of the Skull, those hands that had held so many as his majestic voice had restored them, hands that so often had been used to impart a healing touch, were cruelly nailed to a cross.

From that cross the dying Saviour's thoughts are still for others. His first recorded words while being crucified are a prayer for those who have nailed him there. His second saying is directed to one of the thieves nailed either side of him, one who, conscious of the worthiness of his punishment, turned to the Saviour in that very last moment of his life. He found assurance of forgiveness and a place in Paradise. Then, thirdly, the Saviour graciously provides a home and a son for his weeping mother, so faithful at the foot of the cross, from which most of the disciples are noticeably absent.

And as the darkness puts on open display the separation of God the Father and Son, it is another psalm of David, Psalm 22, that provides our Lord with his fourth saying from the cross. Matthew tells us:

> And about the ninth hour Jesus cried out with a loud voice, saying 'Eli, Eli, lama sabachthani?' that is, 'My God, my God, why have you forsaken me?'
>
> (Matthew 27:46)

We know that the Father had forsaken the Son so that he might accept us, clothed in the righteousness and perfect obedience of the Sin-bearer. This same Psalm 22 is again clearly in mind as our Lord cries out in thirst.

But it is his sixth saying that is again uttered with a loud voice. Both Matthew and Mark record that he cried out loudly on a second occasion, and Luke tells us that it was before he uttered his seventh and final cry from the cross, when he committed his spirit into his Father's hands. It is left to John to tell us the substance of that sixth saying of the Saviour.

The previous loud cry had been drawn from the first verse of Psalm 22. This second loud cry takes us to its last verse. As David peered forward, straining to see the substance of what he was writing, he concluded his most Messianic of compositions with the simple phrase, 'He has done this.'

On Calvary, great David's greater Son did do it. He paid the penalty for sin. He bore in his own body our sins. He endured the wrath of Almighty God. He died, the just for the unjust. He laid down his life that we might live. He fulfilled all the types and shadows of the ceremonial law. He poured out his soul unto death, and was numbered with the transgressors. He therefore had the right to cry with a loud voice,

> It is finished!
> (John 19:30)

What happened at that moment? The great Christmas Evans, perhaps the mightiest preacher in Wales of the last two centuries, sums it up in his inimitable way:

> That moment Justice dropped his flaming sword at the foot of the cross; and the law joined the prophets in witnessing to 'the righteousness which is by faith', for all heard the dying Redeemer exclaim, in triumph, 'It is finished!'
>
> The weeping church heard it, and lifting up her head, cried, 'It is finished!' The attending angels caught the shout of victory, and winged their flight to the eternal throne, singing, 'It is finished!' The powers of darkness heard the acclamations of the universe, and hurried away from the scene in all the agony of disappointment and despair; for the bond was paid, and eternal redemption obtained.[9]

Those loud exclamations remind us that they were uttered not from a body defeated by death, but by One who was willingly giving himself up, not so much a victim of the cross as a Victor over it. They remind us too that

> The voice of the LORD is powerful;
> The voice of the LORD is full of majesty.

6
Splintered cedars

'The voice of the LORD breaks the cedars,
Yes, the LORD splinters the cedars of Lebanon.
He makes them also skip like a calf,
Lebanon and Sirion like a young wild ox.
The voice of the LORD divides the flames of fire.'
(Psalm 29:5-7)

The books that are written today come to life in a different way from all those authored in the last few centuries. Gone are the days of the writer sitting at his desk scribbling away with pencil and paper, and making good use of an eraser as he hones and sharpens each sentence to portray his exact meaning. Now a word processor, complete with well-used backspace and delete keys, is the standard tool!

But that does not mean that the pencil has outlived its usefulness. It has been calculated that approximately fifteen billion pencils are sold worldwide every year. When you realise that the average pencil, costing just a few pence and capable of being carried in the top pocket or behind an ear, can draw a line thirty-five miles long, or write around 45,000 words if sharpened the average seventeen times, you can see why it will long be the world's favourite writing instrument. You may know that the USA's annual pencil supply, laid end to end, would circle the earth ten times, and that most people, apparently, prefer yellow pencils; but, like me, you probably do not know why, whenever you need one, you can never find one! There must surely be a giant sofa somewhere, down the back of which they all disappear!

Historically most pencils have been made from cedar wood. The usual American pencil is made from Pacific Coast cedar, clay from the state of Georgia, Brazilian carnuba wax, a Middle Eastern gum called tragacanth, and Madagascan graphite. The average cedar tree produces enough wood for 172,000 pencils which, added together, could draw a line that would be—well, very long indeed!

No doubt, extremely precise and well-sharpened machines are used to cut up the cedars for pencil production. But David knows of a faster way to shred cedar, and as he watches the storm at his height he tells us about it:

> The voice of the LORD breaks the cedars,
> Yes, the LORD splinters the cedars of Lebanon.

The storm has rolled in from the Mediterranean and has struck the northern part of the kingdom with a fearsome intensity. First in its path are Lebanon and Sirion (the name given here and elsewhere in Scripture to Mount Hermon). The thunderbolts and the lightning, for this seems to be the most likely meaning of these verses, cut through even Lebanon's cedars with incredible ease.

The cedars of Lebanon are spoken of frequently throughout Scripture. The wood from these large spreading coniferous trees, which sadly are not found in any great number in the area nowadays, was widely sought after in Bible times. It was regarded as exceptionally durable, and so found its way into all the best building projects. Both David's house and, more importantly, God's house, Solomon's temple, made good use of the then abundant raw material. The new temple, built after the return from exile, also used cedar logs from Lebanon, even though the finished building was nowhere near as outwardly grand as its predecessor.

Because of their fame, the cedars of Lebanon were used figuratively in Scripture, and, no doubt, elsewhere. Cedars often reach a height of some forty metres, and so the Old Testament writers sometimes used them when describing the stature of man. The Psalmist uses the picture as he thinks of the standing of a righteous man:

> The righteous shall flourish like a palm tree,
> He shall grow like a cedar in Lebanon.
> Those who are planted in the house of the LORD
> Shall flourish in the courts of our God.
>
> (Psalm 92:12-13)

But in this psalm David shows us that, grand and exalted though the cedar may be, it is no match for the power of God as displayed by the storm. Or rather, the power of God easily turns it into match!

It is the apostle James who tells us about the forest fire and the ease with which a small fire can reap destruction in its wake:

> See how great a forest a little fire kindles.
>
> (James 3:5)

Watch any summer news bulletins from forestry areas in the United States or Australia, and you will see how even a single lightning strike is dreaded by those living in wooded areas.

On 20 May 1998, a concerned householder rang the emergency services to say that she could see smoke on St Ignace Island, which is located in Nipigon Bay, in the southern part of Canada. An air surveillance reported the fire to be 1.5 hectares in size. The tinder-dry conditions, following a warm and dry spring in the area, coupled with north-east winds, meant that within two hours the fire covered 65 hectares. Within two days, the fire, which had started with one simple lightning strike, covered 200 hectares, and 1,900 hectares just another two days later. By the time heavy rain fell, a further five days later, over 2,500 hectares had been destroyed, that is, over 15 per cent of the island. Couple a lightning strike with high winds, and it is easy to see how a whole forest of even cedarwood, previously standing so tall and proud, can be humbled by the power of God.

Perhaps that is why other Old Testament writers used the same picture when they described God's ability to destroy his enemies. In Isaiah 2, the great prophet uses the picture when speaking of the day of God's judgement:

> For the day of the LORD of hosts
> Shall come upon everything proud and lofty,
> Upon everything lifted up—
> And it shall be brought low—
> Upon all the cedars of Lebanon that are high and lifted up . . .
>
> (Isaiah 2:12-13a)

Or listen to God's words recorded by Amos the prophet:

> Yet it was I who destroyed the Amorite before them,
> Whose height was like the height of the cedars,
> And he was as strong as the oaks;
> Yet I destroyed his fruit above
> And his roots beneath.
>
> (Amos 2:9)

Such an idea would sit nicely in David's memory. He would think back to that day when he was still a boy, the day he first sprang to public prominence. Yes, he had already been set apart by God, and anointed by his prophet Samuel. It was on that day, however, the day that a nine-foot giant, an uncircumcised Philistine, had dared to challenge David's God and his people, that David first came to King Saul's attention. And it was on that day that he had first earned the love of the people who would one day sing of his victories.

He would remember that moment when he took those five smooth stones from the brook and, facing the goading and mocking of his opponent, pronounced that he came to the battle-field

> in the name of the LORD of hosts, the God of the armies of Israel, whom you have defied.
>
> (1 Samuel 17:45)

He would call to mind the earth-shaking thud that accompanied the fall of that cedar of Philistia, and the gratifying sight of thousands of Goliath's compatriots, on seeing their champion decapitated, running for their lives! Yes, indeed,

> The voice of the LORD breaks the cedars,
> Yes, the LORD splinters the cedars of Lebanon.

And God still downs such proud and exalted men, and some-times during storms too. How grateful God's people have been down the centuries for that storm that raged over the Atlantic Ocean on the night of 10 March 1748, when a slave-ship captain was washed from his bunk, even as the ship he was sailing on appeared to breaking up amidst eighty-mile-an-hour winds and towering waves. On that day, a man whose godly upbringing by a devout woman had largely been erased by the haze of alcohol and immorality that now characterised his life, was brought face to face with death and eternity. The Word of God, so impressed in his mind as a youth, had become nothing more than the sub-ject of his coarser songs. Now, however, those verses of Scripture flashed back into his mind, and he found himself call-ing for mercy to the God whose name he had so often profaned. That man, John Newton, went on to write:

> Amazing grace! how sweet the sound!
>   That saved a wretch like me!
> I once was lost, but now am found;
>   Was blind, but now I see.

Yes, David was right.

> The voice of the LORD breaks the cedars,
> Yes, the LORD splinters the cedars of Lebanon.

Is there a cedar of Lebanon in your life? Someone perhaps that you have prayed for, maybe over many years? Someone who stands tall and proud against the command to repentance that the gospel brings? Take courage! Pray on! Remember what David tells us here!

As these verses progress, David continues to portray the effects of the storm on the created order. It is not just the forest-covered mountains of Lebanon that are visibly shaken, but Mount Hermon also. Perhaps he is describing the crash of the thunderbolts making the earth seem to quake. That is how he will speak of the effect of the storm on the wilderness of Kadesh in the next verse. Or maybe David is describing the visual effect created by the frequent flashes of lightning, which appear to make the hills and mountains dance like young animals. The only thing that punctuates the lightning display are the peals of thunder, for as he says,

> The voice of the LORD divides the flames of fire.

For Mount Hermon to be shaken, whether in reality or only in appearance, was quite something. It was easily the highest in the region of Palestine, forming as it did the northern boundary of Israel's conquests from the Amorites, as recorded in the book of Joshua. Snow usually lay at its summit all the year round, and when that melted it provided icy streams which fed the River Jordan. Its heavy dews enabled it to stand out against the parched background of the region. No doubt, that is why David returned to Mount Hermon for an illustration when he wrote that beautiful psalm on the unity of God's people:

> Behold how good and how pleasant it is
> For brethren to dwell together in unity! . . .

It is like the dew of Hermon,
Descending upon the mountains of Zion;
For there the LORD commanded the blessing—
Life for evermore.

(Psalm 133:1,3)

Hermon was regarded as a sacred place by the Canaanites who had originally inhabited the land. It was, to them, Baal-Hermon (Judges 3:3). So perhaps David has something else in mind when he describes the effect of the storm on the mountain. In later days God, through Elijah, would defeat Baal, the storm-god of his day, on another mountain, Carmel, and he would do so by sending fire from heaven. And just as Elijah would emphasise that victory by praying for the storm that followed, so the Psalmist is reminding us that his God is the one who brooks no rivals, and refuses to share his glory with another.

For, as Michael Wilcock writes in his commentary on this psalm:

> The real thunder God is not some third-rate Baal but the Judge of the world and the Saviour of the church. By the voice of the storm Psalm 29 calls His people to recognise, praise and obey Him as such.[10]

Yes, it is God who controls the lightning. As the Psalmist tells us elsewhere, it belongs to him and is sent by him:

His lightnings light the world;
The earth sees and trembles.

(Psalm 97:4)

That truth is even more clearly seen in that great section of Job, where God speaks to the patriarch out of the whirlwind:

Who has divided a channel for the overflowing water,
Or a path for the thunderbolt,

69

To cause it to rain on a land where there is no one,
A wilderness in which there is no man . . .?
Can you send out lightnings, that they may go,
And say to you, 'Here we are!'?

(Job 38:25,26,35)

Though scientists have only recently 'discovered' that when lightning strikes the earth, it does so by sending its deadly current along a path that appears a split second before, the truth is that God had spoken to Job about the path for the thunderbolt thousands of years ago! How slow science is to catch up with the Scriptures!

The Lord Jesus spoke about the lightning when he was on earth. Talking about the appearance of false Christs and the arising of false prophets, producing signs and wonders and, but for God's fatherly care, deceiving the elect, he contrasted those events with his own return to this earth:

For as the lightning comes from the east and flashes to the west, so also will the coming of the Son of Man be.

(Matthew 24:27)

In days when hardly a month goes by without the press reporting somebody who has come from nowhere claiming to be the Son of God, and in an age when the church is beset by those claiming to be prophets with a new revelation, that is a verse we should always keep in mind. But when the Son of Man really does return to this earth, we will not need the press to alert us to his arrival!

Although the Lord did speak of lightning, perhaps the most telling link between this Psalm and the New Testament is found in reference to the Day of Pentecost. It was on a very different day, and in a very different context, when there was a new conjunction of divided flames of fire, a mighty rushing wind, and the voice of the LORD speaking. That would be a most fanciful link, were it not for the fact that, according to the Talmud—a Jewish book outlining the laws and practices of the Old Testament people of God—this psalm was appointed to be read at the Feast of Pentecost! It seems possible that the early church saw the events described in Acts 2 as the fulfilment of this psalm.[11]

There were many proud 'cedars of Lebanon' listening to Peter as he stood up to preach that day. Yes, there were people from all over the known world, each of whom, to their amazement, was able to hear the glad tidings of the gospel preached to them in their own tongue. But there were also Jewish leaders, men of Judea, whom the apostle, transformed and anointed by the Holy Ghost, was able to fearlessly challenge:

Men of Israel, hear these words: Jesus of Nazareth, a man attested by God to you by miracles, wonders and signs which God did through him in your midst, as you yourselves also know—him, being delivered by the carefully planned intention and foreknowledge of God, you have taken by lawless hands, have crucified, and put to death; whom God raised up . . .

(Acts 2:22-24)

Peter spoke to them of this Jesus, and of his atoning death and resurrection. Accusingly, yet lovingly, he reminded them of the part they had played in the crucifixion of the One of whom David, the psalmist whose compositions they were singing at that Feast, had written so often. Indeed, in his sermon the apostle quotes from at least three of those psalms, ending on the triumphant note of the ascension, looked forward to by David himself:

The LORD said to my Lord,
'Sit at my right hand,
Till I make your enemies your footstool.'
(Acts 2:34-35)

This Jesus, Peter says, 'God has made . . . both Lord and Christ.' At this point the haughty cedars listening to the sermon are broken, turned to splinters or, to use Luke's words, 'cut to the heart' by the voice of the Lord.

To their cry of 'Men and brethren, what shall we do?' comes Peter's reply:

> Repent, and let every one of you be baptized in the name of Jesus Christ for the remission of sins; and you shall receive the gift of the Holy Spirit.
>
> (Acts 2:38)

About three thousand souls were added to the church that day! They included people from every nation where a Jewish community existed, people who went back to declare to their own country and in their 'own tongues the wonderful works of God' (Acts 2:11). But they also included mountainous men of Israel, men for whom, as Luke has told us in his earlier volume, the Saviour prayed even as they crucified him,

> Father, forgive them, for they do not know what they do.
>
> (Luke 23:34)

The Saviour's prayer had been answered! David's psalm had been fulfilled:

> The voice of the LORD breaks the cedars,
> Yes, the LORD splinters the cedars of Lebanon.
> He makes them also skip like a calf,
> Lebanon and Sirion like a young wild ox.
> The voice of the LORD divides the flames of fire.

7
Shaken and stirred!

The voice of the Lord shakes the wilderness;
The Lord shakes the Wilderness of Kadesh.
The voice of the Lord makes the deer give birth,
And strips the forests bare;
And in his temple everyone says, 'Glory!'
(Psalm 29:8-9)

The Christmas season of 2003 was overshadowed by news of a terrible disaster. On Boxing Day, the ancient town of Bam in southern Iran was virtually destroyed by a powerful earthquake. Over 30,000 people were killed. The often rudimentary structure of their mud and brick houses provided little protection against one of the most fearful of natural disasters. The world mourned.

Christians had particular reason to share in the sorrow. It emerged that at the exact moment the quake struck, twenty-eight Christians were gathered for a prayer meeting in the town. All of them were killed as the earth shook and the house collapsed. They had been members of the first recognised church to have existed in the area for more than six centuries. It seemed a severe blow to the church in Iran as a whole, surviving as it had amidst years of persecution of its leaders by a hostile government. How inscrutable are the ways of the Lord!

Living in the United Kingdom, we have little experience of earthquakes. We find the occasional earth tremor that rattles the cups on our kitchen shelves and topples the odd chimney-pot, unsettling enough. When we see, on the television news, the record of the event, the lines on the seismologist's graph seem quite impressive—that is, until we compare it to a graph for an earthquake in Turkey or San Francisco, or even that one in Iran. How terrifying it must be really to feel the ground shake!

As David continues to write about the storm in this psalm, it is to an earthquake that he likens its effects. Some commentators have thought that the storm was actually accompanied by an earthquake, but it does not seem necessary to go as far as that. Anyone who has been in a house with a thunderstorm going on overhead will testify that sometimes it feels as if the ground is moving, such is the force of the thunderclaps. That is what is probably happening here.

The storm has obviously moved south in its path of destruction across Israel. In David's estimation it is now over the Wilderness of Kadesh. Kadesh marked the southernmost part of the kingdom, and so provides a fitting counterpoint to Lebanon and Hermon, which he has mentioned in the previous verses. The storm, David says, has power even to shake the vast Wilderness of Kadesh.

Kadesh has a rich scriptural history. Its first mention in the Bible is found among reports of the battles between kings in the time of Lot, way back in Genesis 14. Then, a few chapters later, it is brought to our attention again in the narrative of the fugitive Hagar's experience of God.

However, it is with the exodus of God's people from Egypt that Kadesh really takes its place in the history of Israel. On more than one occasion on the journey through the wilderness from Sinai, the people stayed in the region of Kadesh (see Numbers 13:26; 20:1; Deuteronomy 1:19,46). It was from this area that Moses sent the spies into Canaan; and so it was in this region too that the people doubted the word of the spies, and indeed the promise of God, and were condemned to another forty years of wilderness wanderings.

At Kadesh also, as recorded in Numbers 20, Miriam died and was buried, and Moses struck the rock, failing to glorify God in so doing. For this he paid a heavy price:

Then the LORD spoke to Moses and Aaron, 'Because you did not believe me, to hallow me in the eyes of the children of Israel, therefore you shall not bring this congregation into the land which I have given them.'

(Numbers 20:12)

In the books of both Joshua and Ezekiel, Kadesh is earmarked as the southern boundary-point of the territory of Judah.

A study that is even more interesting is that of the earthquakes of Scripture! We have already referred to the thunderings and lightnings of Mount Sinai. But we should never forget that these things were accompanied by the quaking of the earth too. In another of his psalms David tells us:

O God, when you went out before your people,
When you marched through the wilderness,   Selah
The earth shook;
The heavens also dropped rain at the presence of God;
Sinai itself was moved at the presence of God, the God of
    Israel.

(Psalm 68:7-8)

The wilderness wanderings also provide us with a further example of an earthquake. The occasion is recorded in Numbers 16, when Korah, Dathan and Abiram were swallowed up in God's righteous judgement of their sin.

Then in 1 Samuel 14 we read of the time that Jonathan and his armour-bearer attacked the garrison at Gibeah. We are told:

And there was trembling in the camp, in the field, and among all the people. The garrison and the raiders also trembled; and the earth quaked, so that it was a very great trembling.

(1 Samuel 14:15)

A few verses later we read of what happened as a result:

So the LORD saved Israel that day . . .

(1 Samuel 14:23)

Perhaps the most famous instance of the earth quaking in the Old Testament, however, was when the Lord spoke to Elijah at Horeb, as recorded for us in 1 Kings 19. God had told Elijah to stand on the mountain before the Lord.

> And behold, the LORD passed by, and a great and strong wind tore into the mountains and broke the rocks in pieces before the LORD, but the LORD was not in the wind; and after the wind an earthquake, but the LORD was not in the earthquake; and after the earthquake a fire, but the LORD was not in the fire; and after the fire a still small voice.
>
> (1 Kings 19:11-12)

What is clear from all these passages is that Old Testament earthquakes are not just random events, quirks of the natural world, but, like the thunder and lightning, they are under the control of Almighty God. They often signify God's action, frequently in judgement, sometimes in the salvation of his people. Indeed, it is for the salvation of God's people that he must enter into judgement with those who rebel against him.

The joining of judgement through earthquake to thunder and lightning is seen in another of David's psalms:

> The LORD also thundered in the heavens,
> And the Most High uttered his voice,
> Hailstones and coals of fire.
> He sent out his arrows and scattered the foe,
> Lightnings in abundance, and he vanquished them.
> Then the channels of waters were seen,
> And the foundations of the world were uncovered
> At your rebuke, O LORD,
> At the blast of the breath of your nostrils.
>
> (Psalm 18:13-15)

When we come to consider the earthquakes of the New Testament, we must bear in mind the sovereignty of God in the earthquake, and the fact that it signifies that *he* is at work. There are probably three that come to mind.

The first of these occurs at the crucifixion of the Saviour. Matthew tells us of the moment that he died:

> Jesus, when he had cried out again with a loud voice, yielded up his spirit. And behold, the veil of the temple was torn in two from top to bottom; and the earth quaked, and the rocks were split . . . Now when the centurion and those with him, who were guarding Jesus, saw the earthquake and the things that had happened, they feared greatly, saying, 'Truly this was the Son of God!'
>
> (Matthew 27:50,51,54)

At the start of that week, Jesus had warned the Pharisees that if the people of Jerusalem were stopped from singing his praise, the stones themselves would cry out (Luke 19:40). The people had stopped, and the voices of the stones and the rocks replaced them.

The earthquake at the cross tells us that *God* is at work. He is at work in the judgement of sin and for the salvation of his people. On the cross, both these wondrous works are accomplished. That is why we must part company with those who tell us every Easter that the cross of Jesus represents the great tragedy of the best of men being silenced by those who did not understand him. We have not understood Calvary at all, unless we have seen that it is the work of Almighty God.

That Passover was an earth-shaking weekend in Jerusalem, for on the first day of the next week another earthquake took place! Again, it is Matthew who tells us about it:

> Now after the Sabbath, as the first day of the week began to dawn, Mary Magdalene and the other Mary came to see the tomb. And behold, there was a great earthquake; for an angel of the Lord descended from heaven, and came and rolled back

the stone from the door, and sat on it . . . And the guards shook for fear of him, and became like dead men.

(Matthew 28:1-2,4)

Let nobody doubt it! God is at work! The sacrifice has been accepted. The One who was delivered up for our transgressions has been raised for our justification.

The salvation he has secured is now applied to all who will believe on the Lord Jesus Christ. That was what another first-century Roman guard realised, to his eternal benefit, when an earthquake hit his prison workplace as Paul and Silas were singing God's praises and the clock struck midnight. Luke tells us in Acts 16 that 'the foundations of the prison were shaken'. More importantly, the foundations of that man were shaken. Indeed, from that moment on he had a proper foundation for the first time, the Lord Jesus Christ, God's only Son. Luke tells us that 'all the doors were opened and everyone's chains were loosed'. More significantly, the door of that jailer's hard heart had been opened, and the chains that kept him under the power of sin and Satan had been shattered. The voice of the Lord that shook the wilderness of Kadesh had shaken this man, and before long he was a founder member of the church at Philippi.

The Bible forewarns us that one day the universe will shake again:

But the day of the Lord will come as a thief in the night, in which the heavens will pass away with a great noise, and the elements will melt with fervent heat; both the earth and the works that are in it will be burned up.

(2 Peter 3:10}

That day, too, will be marked by the twin themes of judgement and salvation.

The next verse of our psalm records for us a threefold effect of 'the voice of the LORD' shaking the earth. Firstly,

The voice of the LORD makes the deer give birth . . .

All nature is dominated by the storm. Terrified animals are shocked into premature labour. Just as the book of Job tells us that God is the One who sets the time for the deer to calve (Job 39:1-4), so the voice of the Lord is deemed responsible here. If people are not moved by the storm, the animals are. As David Dickson quaintly commented three hundred and fifty years ago:

> Whence learn . . . that the stupidity and senselessness of man is greater than that of brute creatures, which are all more moved with the thunder, than the hearts of men for the most part, as here may be seen in the comparison.[12]

The second effect recorded is that the voice of the LORD

> . . . strips the forests bare.

The combined effect of the heavy rain and hail, and perhaps of accompanying wind, is the denuding of the trees. Maybe, as David surveyed this result of the storm, his mind went back to another story from his Old Testament history, when thunder and hail had caused similar natural destruction. For that we must go back to the land of bondage.

Six plagues had come and gone as God sent punishment upon the Egyptians for refusing to submit to God's demand for the freedom of his people. Pharoah had simply hardened his heart, and as he did so, the Lord had hardened Pharaoh's heart too. The seventh plague God promised would be of 'hail . . . such as has not been in Egypt since its founding until now'. Then we read:

> And Moses stretched out his rod towards heaven; and the LORD sent thunder and hail, and fire darted to the ground. And the LORD rained hail on the land of Egypt . . . And the hail struck throughout the whole land of Egypt, all that was in the field, both man and beast; and the hail struck every herb of the field and broke every tree of the field.
>
> (Exodus 9:23,25)

Even that seventh plague did not soften Pharoah's heart, and neither would the eighth nor ninth. It would take the death of his firstborn to do that, and even then only temporarily. But the death of Pharoah's firstborn meant deliverance for God's people. The death of God's only begotton Son, the Firstborn over all creation, would be necessary to procure our salvation.

The third effect of the storm described in the ninth verse is perhaps the most uplifting:

> And in his temple everyone says, 'Glory!'

This central section of the psalm, which has begun with a description of God as 'The God of glory', draws to its close with an earthly recognition of the same glory from those gathered together to worship this glorious God. Though, of course, the temple in Jerusalem had yet to be constructed, David here and elsewhere in the Psalms talks of the place where God's people gathered for his worship. We know that such places existed. We might cast our minds back to the annual pilgrimages to Shiloh, which the story of Hannah and her request for a son illustrates.

David imagines the response to the storm of the gathered people of God. The storm that has shaken the earth has stirred God's people. It is interesting to note that he had no doubt that God's people would still be at worship, despite the inclement weather! How many ministers have risen from their bed on a Sunday morning, drawn back the curtain to see pouring rain, and turned to their wives saying, 'There won't be many in church this morning'! How sad it is that those who shop in the rain on Friday, and play sport in the rain on Saturday, must stay at home because of rain on the Lord's Day!

No, God's people are in his house, about his business. And their response to the voice of the Lord and the power and magnificence that it has displayed is a simple one: 'Glory!'

And of course, that is, in a word, what we gather together as God's people to do. We do not come to worship simply to sing songs, or even to hear the Bible read. Far less should we come to see each other and to catch up on the news of the past week. We come to worship Almighty God. We come to tell God that he is glorious. We come, as David has already reminded us, to

> Give unto the LORD glory and strength.
> Give unto the LORD the glory due to his name.

That demands preparation. It demands concentration. It demands consecration. But anything else cannot be true worship.

Of course, there are times when God so breaks into the worship of his people that we can do nothing else but exclaim, 'Glory!' Such times were known in the Wales of three centuries ago. God was mightily blessing the land through the preaching of Daniel Rowland, Howel Harris and others. It was, arguably, the most powerful revival the Principality has ever seen. Although it happened well before the time of tape recordings or television broadcasts, we have many powerful eyewitness testimonies to the meetings. Their vibrancy means that we can almost be seated in the pews as the preaching is heard!

One such account has come down to us from a man by the name of Robert Jones, from Caernarvonshire.[13] He was accustomed to walking eighty miles, whatever the weather, to hear Daniel Rowland in his home church in Llangeitho. He tells us that although he was tired when he got there, before Rowland had preached for ten minutes, all was forgotten and he felt amply repaid. That was true of all the congregation, who would be sitting in rapt attention as, mightily empowered by the Holy Spirit, Rowland expounded some text, perhaps John 3:16. Jones tells us that the preacher

> gave a graphic description of the everlasting love of God, and set forth the infinite glory of the Person of the Son of God; he dwelt upon the depths of His sufferings, and the infinite value of His sacrifice, until this man was absolutely lost in marvel

and wonder, and knew not whether he was in the body or not, whether he was in heaven or on earth.

Jones was not the only one to feel that way. The congregation were

all in riveted attention, deep absorption, and intense delight. Sometimes they would break out in loud expressions of praise to God for his love: *Gogoniant*!

Gogoniant! This is the Welsh word for 'Glory to God!' It is as David imagined it in this psalm.

How much, as God's people, we need a sight of his glory! How great is our need for him to visit us again, as he did in the days of Daniel Rowland! O that we might hear the voice of God, the voice which shakes men out of their sinful apathy towards spiritual things, that strips them of their proud self-trust, and that brings them to new birth by the mighty work of his Holy Spirit! We need to hear God's voice again, because

> The voice of the LORD shakes the wilderness;
> The LORD shakes the wilderness of Kadesh.
> The voice of the LORD makes the deer give birth,
> And strips the forests bare;
> And in his temple everyone says, 'Glory!'

8
The eternal King

'The LORD sat enthroned at the Flood,
And the LORD sits as King for ever.'
(Psalm 29:10)

The people of Wales, like all other nations, have a rich cultural heritage. That is expressed in every area of the arts, perhaps most notably at the annual Eisteddfod, a gathering held every summer in a different part of Wales. There, a giant celebration of the Welsh language, its poetry, song and dance takes place, drawing people from all over the Principality, and from pockets of exiled Welsh living all over the world.

Part of that cultural heritage takes the form of legends that have been told to generations of children. One such story is about a couple called Dwyfan and Dwyfach. According to the tale, the lake Llion one day burst its banks, overflowing the land. Everybody was drowned except for Dwyfan and Dwyfach; they survived in a mastless ship, with pairs of every living animal, and eventually landed in *Prydain*, now Britain!

Does that story sound familiar to you? It would do if you were a Lithuanian. There is a legend in Lithuanian folklore about the god Pramzimas, who sent two giants, Wandu and Wejas, to flood the earth. Only a few people survived, including an elderly couple, together with some animals. They did so by floating in a nutshell, which the god had accidentally dropped. After the flood, Pramzimas sent a rainbow to comfort them.

Or perhaps you are Alaskan. Well, in that case, you might know an ancient story that your people tell, about how the father of their ancestors was one day warned that a great flood was coming to destroy the earth. He built a raft, and so was able to save himself, his family and some animals. The animals complained about the long time they had to spend on the raft, and so when the flood abated they lost their ability to speak as a punishment.

I think you might be getting the picture! In fact, it has been calculated that over two hundred people groups around the world have flood narratives as part of their traditions.[14] Though each has its regional variation, they nearly all involve a small number of people who are saved, with animals, in a boat, from a flood which affects the whole world. In many of these stories the flood comes from the god(s), who are angry at people's wrongdoing, and in the majority of them the boat ends up stuck on a mountain.

That should not surprise Christians who believe the whole Bible, including the first chapters of Genesis. If the story of Noah is true, and every person and people group are descended from him, we might expect such an event to have been recounted by succeeding generations of every culture. Man's natural invention, and his sinful bias away from God, would lead us to recognise that the story is likely to change over time. You only have to play 'Chinese Whispers' at a party to see that! But the existence of flood stories on every continent of the world is a testimony to the veracity of that which many Christian people are happy to deny.

Not that we should believe the story of Noah just because of these legends. We believe, first and foremost, because God's Word is true. Even if there were no secondary evidence, the Bible is still God's truth. Christians have believed in the stories of Shadrach, Meshach, Abednego, Daniel, Nebuchadnezzar and Belshazzar ever since they were written down. Only recently has archaeological evidence emerged which so clearly underlines the trustworthiness of the scriptural record. We don't believe because the world verifies, but *before* it does so. The Bible believer has nothing to fear from the discoveries of history, or science, or genetics, or anything else. God's Word is true!

The truth of the story of Noah and the Flood is underlined by the references to it elsewhere in Scripture. In the Old Testament it is mentioned by the Chronicler, by Isaiah, and by Ezekiel. In the New, we read of it in the letter to the Hebrews, and in both of Peter's epistles, as well as in the Gospels, for Jesus obviously believed Noah to be a real man, and the Flood an historical event.

And here in Psalm 29 we read of the Flood, as the thunderstorm has moved out of the country and everything is returning to peaceful normality. Some commentators have suggested that David is not referring to the Great Flood here, but just to the effects of the recently concluded tempest (or even to the state of affairs described in Genesis 1:2). But there is compelling evidence to make us believe that they are wrong. The Old Testament has nine different Hebrew words that are translated in the Authorised Version by the English word 'flood'. The word used exclusively in the Flood narrative in Genesis 6–9 is the Hebrew word *mabbul,* and this word is used in only one other place in the Old Testament. Guess where! Yes, here in Psalm 29:9. David has deliberately chosen his word from the thesaurus available to him! He wants to focus our attention on that cataclysmic event of history.

Perhaps the storm had lasted so long that David had begun to wonder whether it was going to rain for forty days and nights. Perhaps as he surveys its devastating effects, as described in the previous verses, he has begun to think of what happened in the days of Noah. Or perhaps, as he concludes the psalm, he notices that the dark thunderclouds have been replaced by a brilliant rainbow. We cannot tell. But either way, his thoughts are taken to the Flood, and to the God who sat enthroned above it.

And as the storm rumbles away into the distance, it is on that aspect of the Great Flood that he focuses. The tempest has done its worst. It has caused fear in the hearts of men, and devastation to the natural world in its path. But it is over. It has ended, as storms always do. That is true in the meteorological world, and it is true of the storms of life. Storms only hold temporary sway, but God is sovereign. He is on the throne, just as he was throughout Noah's time.

In the references to the Flood in the rest of Scripture (as noted on page 85), our focus is directed to different aspects of that event. Ezekiel, for example, likens Noah to Job and Daniel in terms of righteousness, and shows by comparison the sinfulness of the children of Israel. Isaiah, on the other hand, uses it, and the covenant promise made to Noah at its end, to emphasise just how trustworthy God is. Peter, in his epistles, demonstrates through it the long-suffering patience of God, and also the fact that he will not always be patient with man. Just as he brought judgement upon the earth with flood waters, even as the people mocked Noah, saying it would never happen, so one day God will purge his creation by fire.

But here, in this psalm, it is clear that the Flood is meant to point us to something else. 'The LORD' reigns, and because of that he 'sat enthroned at the Flood'. When we think about it, there is much about the sovereign rule of God displayed in the Flood.

First, we should remember that the Flood occurred because God's sovereignty was being challenged. It happened because

> the LORD saw that the wickedness of man was great in the earth, and that every intent of the thoughts of his heart was only evil continually.
>
> (Genesis 6:5)

Sin is always an act of rebellion against a holy God. He is sovereign. He has laid down the way in which we should live upon his earth, both in his law and on our consciences. Every act of sin is a refusal to submit to that sovereignty, a refusal that, by nature, makes us enemies of God. How God's people should remember that! O that we had our Puritan forefathers' view of the sinfulness of sin!

Into that situation the sovereign Lord makes a sovereign decision:

> I will destroy man whom I have created from the face of the earth.
>
> (Genesis 6:7)

That decision was one that no one could contradict. The LORD was sitting enthroned.

But then, wonderfully, we see sovereign grace! God's grace is always sovereign. How wonderful it is to read in the next verse:

> But Noah found grace in the eyes of the LORD.

What is even more thrilling to see, is that Noah's receiving of God's grace precedes the description of him in the next verse. He doesn't find grace because he is 'a just man, perfect in his generations'. That is never God's way. Grace is undeserved. It must be, otherwise it would be reward, not grace. And grace is sovereign grace!

Do you regularly stop to thank God for his sovereign grace in your life? Do you ever do so? Without grace there could be no salvation, no justification, no sanctification, no adoption, no imputed righteousness, no hope of heaven. Without grace, there would have been no sacrificed Son on Calvary's cross.

The Flood shows God's sovereignty in other ways too. Take the covenant that God introduces to Noah as he instructs him in the building of the ark. Every time God talks in covenant with man, throughout the Scriptures, it is God who sets the terms. It is not like the agreements man makes with man. There can be no give-and-take, no haggling about conditions. We should be amazed that God could ever make promises to his creatures! It is all of grace that he does! But he sets the terms. He has the right to demand covenant-faithfulness, for he is sovereign.

There is more evidence of the truth of David's statement in this verse when we turn to Genesis chapter 7. How did Noah collect all those animals from all over the known world? That is the question so often asked by the sceptics, the same sceptics who doubt the shutting of the lions' mouths in Daniel's time and the opening of the great fish's mouth in Jonah's. The answer is simple. It is David's answer:

The LORD sat enthroned at the flood.

There is not one animal that Noah has to go looking for. His job is to build the ark and warn the people. God will bring the animals. And he does, because he is sovereign.

Then there is another evidence of God's sovereignty. In chapter 7:16 we read a few short words that carry a weight of importance:

. . . and the LORD shut him in.

What a display of sovereignty! God didn't leave the shutting of the door to Noah. If he had, Noah would not have been safe. When the Lord shuts the door, those inside are truly secure. But those outside are truly lost.

The final part of Genesis 7 shows the order with which the disorder of Flood is poured upon the earth. Nothing is happening outside the control of the One who sits enthroned above it. Time and again in these verses we read that 'the water prevailed', but viewing it from the dry land of this psalm we know that 'the voice of the LORD is over the waters'.

Perhaps the most telling illustration of the sovereignty of God over the deluge comes, however, at its end. First, we are told, not that the rains stopped of their own volition, but that

The fountains of the deep and the windows of heaven were also stopped, and the rain from heaven was restrained.

(Genesis 8:2)

The double promise that Jehovah makes to Noah at the end of chapter 8 bears all the hallmarks of One whose reign is secure for eternity. In response to the soothing sweet smell of the sacrifice, God makes a wondrous promise—two promises in fact. First, there will never be a repeat of such devastation. We read:

> Then the LORD said in his heart, 'I will never again curse the ground for man's sake, although the imagination of man's heart is evil from his youth; nor will I again destroy every living thing as I have done.'
>
> (Genesis 8:21)

How is it that God can make such a certain promise? Well, David gives us the answer in the second part of the verse. The storm that is the focus of the psalm has finished. The Flood came to an end too. Other storms will come and go; that is the nature of weather. But one thing is constant. David continues the verse:

> And the LORD sits as King for ever.

Like the weather, nothing in life lasts for ever. At the start of the school holidays it seems to every child that the weeks ahead will never end. But the first day of term soon comes around. Then, to the overworked teacher, the term ahead seems to stretch into infinity!

Ask the newly widowed pensioner, as she buries her husband after sixty years of marriage, and she will say, 'I thought we would always be together!' But change and decay are written into the order of this fallen world.

One thing is eternal, though, and that is the fact that the Lord is King! That he reigns is one of the favourite statements of the Psalmist in particular, and not only in the so-called 'kingship' psalms. The Psalmist tells us:

> The LORD reigns, he is clothed with majesty.
>
> (Psalm 93:1)

Psalms 97 and 98 begin in a similar way, with a ringing acclamation of the sovereignty of God. And that sovereignty is an eternal one.

Because God reigns eternally, he can go on to the second part of the promise to Noah:

> While the earth remains,
> Seedtime and harvest,
> And cold and heat,
> And winter and summer,
> And day and night
> Shall not cease.
> (Genesis 8:22)

Every time you plant a seed in the ground, or celebrate God's goodness at a harvest festival, you are bearing testimony to the truth of David's statement in this verse, that the God who sat enthroned at the Flood, is the LORD who sits as King for ever. Every time you feel the cold of the north wind upon your cheeks, or the rays of the sun burning the skin on your arms, you should rejoice in the same truth. When you turn the clocks back every autumn because winter is coming, and then move them forward an hour the next springtime, you are bearing eloquent testimony to Psalm 29:10. Indeed, the dawning of every day and the falling of every dusk shout loudly:

> The Lord is King; lift up thy voice,
> O earth, and all ye heavens rejoice!
> From world to world the joy shall ring:
> 'The Lord Omnipotent is King!'[15]

In the New Testament, we see that when the Lord Jesus was on earth, he combined preaching about his eternal kingship with a message about the Flood too. In chapter 24 of Matthew's Gospel he tells us:

Heaven and earth will pass away, but my words will by no means pass away. But of that day and hour no one knows, no, not even the angels of heaven, but my Father only. But as the days of Noah were, so also will be the coming of the Son of Man be. For as in the days before the flood, they were eating and drinking, marrying and giving in marriage, until the day that Noah entered the ark, and did not know until the flood came and took them all away, so also will the coming of the Son of Man be.

(Matthew 24:35-39)

The Lord had no doubts about the historic reality of the Flood, or of the person of Noah. They were, he said, a clear warning to the people of every generation. Noah's preaching was ignored by the people of his day. There were other things that were far more important to them: the day-to-day business of preparing meals and planning marriages took priority. And then a day came when they were swept away. On that day everything was swept away. Houses, trees, animals, people—all had no hope in the face of such a torrent. Rocks and mountains that had been permanent since the day of creation were no more. Everything was undermined. Everything but the kingship of the LORD!

Another day is coming, a day that the eternal Son of God said will be just as sudden and unexpected. He is coming back! At that coming there will be no doubt as to his eternal kingship. This time he will not be shrouded in the swaddling cloths of a first-century Jewish stable. Every eye will see him. This time the angels will not simply proclaim his birth, but blow the trumpets and gather in the people of the One whom they accompany on the clouds of glory. This time he will come, not to his own for their rejection, but for his own, to signal their acceptance into the kingdom prepared for them from the foundation of the world.

On that day, the physical globe will be transformed even more drastically than it was in Noah's day:

the heavens will pass away with a great noise, and the elements will melt with fervent heat; both the earth and the works that are in it will be burned up.

(2 Peter 3:10)

Yes, the heavens and earth will pass away, but his words, the Lord Jesus tells us, will not pass away. Why? David has the answer:

> The LORD sat enthroned at the Flood,
> And the LORD sits as King for ever.

9
Strength and peace

'The LORD *will give strength to his people;*
The LORD *will bless his people with peace.'*
(Psalm 29:11)

For once, it had been one of those television dramas that could be watched from beginning to end. There had been no need to reach for the 'off button' because of the content. It had been good family entertainment, and as the characters developed, the story began to draw the viewer into the plot. It was just at that moment when I was beginning to care how the situation would work out that the dreaded words appeared on the screen: 'To be continued'! I looked at the newspaper in disbelief. Yes, it was just 'Part One'. There was more to come, and I was going to have to wait to find out the full story.

There are times when reading David's psalms leaves you with the same feeling! Although each one is a complete piece of inspired poetry, beautiful and challenging in its own right, on occasions there just seems to be more to say. Reading it through New Testament eyes, it seems somehow incomplete. You feel sometimes that you need to add the words, 'To be continued'.

Take Psalm 19, for example. We have looked at it already on beginning our study of this magnificent Psalm 29, and as we come to its end we see another parallel. We noted how David opens Psalm 19 by looking at the sky, describing the wonder of the sun, and exclaiming:

> The heavens declare the glory of God;
> And the firmament shows his handiwork.

93

He spends the first six verses of that fourteen-verse psalm talking about the way God reveals himself in creation around him. But then in the next five verses he describes a second way that God speaks to men and women:

> The law of the LORD is perfect, converting the soul;
> The testimony of the LORD is sure, making wise the simple.
> (Psalm 19:7)

David knew better than anybody that God in his grace had chosen to reveal himself to men and women in his Word. That is why he writes in praise of the Scriptures, both here and in other psalms, and perhaps most notably in Psalm 119.

But living this side of Bethlehem and Nazareth, and especially Calvary, we want the Psalmist to go on and tell us about a third and even greater way in which God has spoken to mankind. As the writer to the Hebrews tells us:

> God, who at various times and in different ways spoke in time past to the fathers by the prophets, has in these last days spoken to us by his Son, whom he has appointed heir of all things, through whom also he made the worlds . . .
> (Hebrews 1:1-2)

David cannot do that, however. He is, as Peter puts it in his first epistle,

> searching what, or what manner of time, the Spirit of Christ who was in them was indicating when he testified beforehand of the sufferings of Christ and the glories that would follow.
> (1 Peter 1:11)

And so Psalm 19 leaves us to think through, from the New Testament, how God has revealed himself in that final, glorious way.

Psalm 29 is like that too. It cries out, 'To be continued'. It calls for us to do some New Testament thinking. And that is what we will aim to do in this chapter.

The storm has rumbled off, out of sight and hearing, and in the post-tempest tranquillity the Psalmist is meditating on the eternal sovereignty of God. Having witnessed the might demonstrated by the storm, he has been thinking about how God used his awesome power to destroy the world of Noah's day. He has pondered how God has kept his covenant promise and not done the same since, even though men and women are equally rebellious now as then. As he concludes the psalm, he does so on a positive note, confident that it is God's intention to use his mighty power for the good of his people:

> The LORD will give strength to his people;
> The LORD will bless his people with peace.
>
> (Psalm 29:11)

Think about those two promised blessings: strength and peace! Examine them with New Testament eyes! Think about them with the mind of the apostle Paul as he writes to the church at Rome:

> Therefore, having been justified by faith, we have peace with God through our Lord Jesus Christ, through whom also we have access by faith into this grace in which we stand, and rejoice in hope of the glory of God . . . For when we were still without strength, in due time Christ died for the ungodly.
>
> (Romans 5:1-2,6)

Did you notice those two words jumping off the page at the reader? Peace and strength! That is what David has promised will be God's blessing. Here, Paul tells us that they have been provided for his people.

And what a chapter in which to introduce them to us! Those first eleven verses of Romans 5 are paying particular attention to what has been achieved for us through the cross of great David's greater Son. They give us a notable fourfold description of what we are before the intervention of the Saviour.

First, in verse 6 the apostle tells us that we are '*ungodly*':

> For when we were still without strength, in due time Christ died for the ungodly.

Everything that God is, we are not! He is perfect in holiness. We are loathsome lawbreakers, set on enthroning ourselves in our lives and rejecting his rule over us.

Secondly, in verse 8 we are described as '*sinners*':

> But God demonstrates his own love towards us, in that while we were still sinners, Christ died for us.

Paul has prefaced that grand description of the Christian message by reminding his readers of how unusual it is for someone to lay down their life for another person, even a person whose lifestyle is exemplary. The thought that a holy God should give his Son, and Christ should give his sinless life, for sinners, is beyond comprehension.

Then in verse 10 we are told that we are '*enemies*' of God:

> For if when we were enemies we were reconciled to God through the death of his Son, much more, having been reconciled, we shall be saved by his life.

Sin is no light matter. Every lawless act is an act of rebellion against Almighty God. It makes him our enemy. It separates us from him. It needs something special to bring about reconciliation.

For the fourth description of our state by nature we return to verse 6, which speaks of our being '*without strength*'. The Greek word that Paul uses here has already appeared several times in the New Testament.

Luke, for example, tells us in his Gospel of a day when Jesus healed a man who was full of leprosy. Over the years in which the leprosy had stealthily taken control of his body, this poor man had been ignored and rejected by friends and neighbours and had been ceremonially unclean. But people's attention was attracted by his healing—and it was an attention that was quickly focused on the Healer:

> Then the report went around concerning him all the more; and great multitudes came together to hear, and to be healed by him of their infirmities.
>
> (Luke 5:15)

The Greek word for 'infirmities' in this verse conveys the same idea as the one word Paul uses for 'without strength'. The scene that confronted the Lord Jesus that day was more heart-rending than the casualty ward of any major hospital. There were the lame and the blind, the deaf and the mute, the paralysed and the haemorrhaging. Also, there were the demon-possessed, and others wrestling with illnesses of a spiritual sort. Such people were written off by Doctor Luke's fellow professionals. They had one thing in common: they were without strength, infirm, unable to do a thing to alleviate, let alone cure, their condition.

Matthew describes a similar occasion in his great eighth chapter. The way he uses this same Greek word is even more revealing:

> When evening had come, they brought to him many who were demon-possessed. And he cast out the spirits with a word, and healed all who were sick, that it might be fulfilled which was spoken by Isaiah the prophet, saying:
>
> '*He himself took our infirmities*
> *And bore our sicknesses.*'
>
> (Matthew 8:16-17)

With that same word for 'infirmity', or being 'without strength', Matthew translates the verse from Isaiah 53, which he regards as fulfilled on that day when the sick gathered in Capernaum. But, from the way this passage is used elsewhere in the New

Testament, we know that this section from Isaiah is talking about the sin-bearing Servant:

> But he was wounded for our transgressions,
> He was bruised for our iniquities;
> The chastisement for our peace was upon him,
> And by his stripes we are healed.
>
> (Isaiah 53:5)

Now we know what David meant when he looked forward at the end of this psalm. He is telling us that Almighty God will use his power to give us strength, to deal with our spiritual infirmity, our helpless inability to come to him and to be saved. How gloriously was that promise fulfilled at Calvary!

The strength-giving of God does not stop there. More real even than the warfare in which David was engaged for so much of his life, is the spiritual battle in which the Christian is summoned to participate. So often the world, the flesh and the devil form an unholy alliance to drag the Christian into sin, and to rob him of the joy of his salvation.

How good it is to read the prayer of the apostle Paul, as he writes to the Ephesians and supplicates God for them,

> that he would grant you, according to the riches of his glory, to be strengthened with might through his Spirit in the inner man . . .
>
> (Ephesians 3:16)

or to read in Peter's first epistle,

> But may the God of all grace, who called us to his eternal glory by Christ Jesus, after you have suffered a while, perfect, establish, strengthen and settle you.
>
> (1 Peter 5:10)

How wonderfully that line of David's psalm is fulfilled! The Lord does give strength to his people!

Peace

What about that blessing of peace, which is promised in the psalm's final line? We all want peace. Ask a resident of the Gaza Strip, or Chechnya, or Belfast, and they will tell you of their longing for peace. Probe the harassed mother dealing with her brood of children, or the elderly couple with the noisy neighbours, and they will ask for the same thing. But the Bible's peace is something far greater than the absence of warfare or the quieting of noise. It is of a different order. It speaks of 'wholeness'. The Lord Jesus said:

> Peace I leave with you, my peace I give to you; not as the world gives do I give to you. Let not your heart be troubled, neither let it be afraid.
>
> (John 14:27)

We need that peace, that wholeness, because of the spiritual brokenness described in that verse in Isaiah 53. We need it, too, because of our enmity against God outlined in the verse in Romans 8. How astonishing it is, therefore, to be able to say with the apostle,

> Therefore, having been justified by faith, we have peace with God through our Lord Jesus Christ.
>
> (Romans 5:1)

But the peace or wholeness that the Lord Jesus Christ came to bring is even wider than that. Not only are we at war with Almighty God, but sin destroys our relationships with our fellow human beings. It is only when we are right with God that this second severed relationship can be healed.

That is a lesson that the Ten Commandments teach us. When God gave his law, amidst the thunder and lightnings on Mount Sinai, he gave us four commandments dealing with our relationship with God, and then a further six regulating our dealings with each other. The not-so-implicit message is that God comes first. Whenever we are far away from him, that will be clearly seen in our family and social life. Over three thousand years of human history provide more empirical evidence than we will ever need to prove that he was right.

The coming of Jesus Christ, therefore, brings peace between man and man too. In his letter to the ethnically mixed church at Ephesus, to a community of Jews and Gentiles who would never have come together without the gospel, the apostle Paul wrote:

> For he himself is our peace, who has made both one, and has broken down the middle wall of division between us, having abolished in his flesh the enmity, that is, the law of commandments contained in ordinances, so as to create in himself one new man from the two, thus making peace, and that he might reconcile them both to God in one body through the cross, thereby putting to death the enmity . . . Now, therefore, you are no longer strangers and foreigners, but fellow citizens with the saints and members of the household of God . . .
>
> (Ephesians 2:14-16,19)

Whilst this book is being written, two notable things are happening in the very places where David ruled. A physical wall is under construction to separate Jew from Palestinian. But at the same time a glorious gospel is being preached, which is breaking down a more real partition and joining together Jew and Arab in praise of the God of Abraham. David was right!

The LORD will bless his people with peace.

That peace has a third dimension, linked indelibly with the first two. Paul wrote about it in his epistle to the Philippians. He pens it from a prison cell, knowing that at any moment the summons to judgement, and then to death, might come. In such a situation he still writes what has become known as the 'letter of joy'. The recipe for such a joy, says the apostle, is not a secret:

> Be anxious for nothing, but in everything by prayer and supplication, with thanksgiving, let your requests be made known to God; and the peace of God, which surpasses all understanding, will guard your hearts and minds through Christ Jesus.
>
> (Philippians 4:6-7)

What is guarding the apostle Paul? The might of Rome might be guarding his body, but the peace of God is guarding his heart and mind, and will guard ours too if we are obedient to the command that precedes such a tremendous promise. Two verses later we read not just of the peace of God, but of the God of peace!

David was so right! God blesses his people with strength and peace because, especially in the person of his Son, and through that Son's atoning death upon Calvary, he has blessed us with himself, the Almighty God, and the God of peace. As we close our study of this glorious psalm, the psalm that began with 'Glory to God in the highest' and ends with 'Peace on earth towards men', we sing in praise with David:

> The LORD will give strength to his people;
> The LORD will bless his people with peace.

Appendix

THOUGH psalms, as part of the Word of God, are to be read and meditated upon, they are also to be sung. We cannot complete our study without letting Psalm 29 warm our souls again through the composition of a hymn-writer who, although he was writing three centuries ago, is still without equal in the history of the church.

Psalm 29

GIVE to the Lord, ye sons of fame,
  Give to the Lord renown and power,
Ascribe due honours to His name,
  And His eternal might adore.

The Lord proclaims His power aloud
  Over the ocean and the land;
His voice divides the wat'ry cloud,
  And lightnings blaze at His command.

He speaks and tempest, hail and wind,
  Lay the wide forest bare around:
The fearful hart and frightened hind
  Leap at the terror of the sound.

To Lebanon He turns His voice,
  And lo, the stately cedars break;
The mountains tremble at the noise,
  The valleys roar, the deserts quake.

The Lord sits sovereign on the flood,
  The Thund'rer reigns for ever king;
But makes His church His blest abode,
  Where we His awful glories sing.

In gentler language there, the Lord
  The counsels of His grace imparts;
Amidst the raging storm, His word
  Speaks peace and courage to our hearts.
Isaac Watts (1674–1748)

The same hymn-writer also composed the following:

The God of Thunder[16]

O THE immense, th'amazing height,
  The boundless grandeur of our God,
Who treads the worlds beneath His feet,
  And sways the nations with His nod!

He speaks, and lo, all nature shakes,
  Heaven's everlasting pillars bow;
He rends the clouds with hideous cracks,
  And shoots his fiery arrows through.

Well let the nations start and fly
  At the blue lightning's horrid glare,
Atheists and emperors shrink and die,
  When flame and noise torment the air.

Let noise and flame confound the skies,
  And drown the spacious realms below,
Yet will we sing the Thunderer's praise,
  And send our loud hosannas through.

Celestial King, Thy blazing power
  Kindles our hearts to flaming joys,
We shout to hear Thy thunders roar,
  And echo to our Father's voice.

Thus shall the God our Saviour come,
  And lightnings round His chariot play:
Ye lightnings, fly to make Him room,
  Ye glorious storms, prepare His way!
Isaac Watts (1674–1748)

References

1. C. H. Spurgeon, *The Treasury of David* (Welwyn, UK, Evangelical Press, 1978), vol. 2, p. 33.
2. J. M. Boice, *Psalms* (Grand Rapids, USA, Baker, 1999), vol. 1, p. 255.
3. From the hymn, 'The Lord Jehovah reigns'.
4. A. M. Harman, *Psalms* (Fearn, Scotland, Christian Focus Publications, 1998), p. 137.
5. From the hymn, 'Praise, my soul, the King of Heaven'.
6. This and similar stories can be found detailed in Billy Graham's book, *Angels: God's Secret Agents* (Waco, Texas, Word, 1986), pp.16,17. Many readers may not endorse everything said in that book, however.
7. G. Grogan, *Prayer, Praise & Prophecy: A Theology of the Psalms* (Fearn, Scotland, Christian Focus Publications, 2001), p. 111.
8. D. Kidner, *Psalms 1–72* (Leicester, England, IVP, 1973), p. 125.
9. Recorded in Owen Jones, *Great Preachers of Wale*s (Clonmel, Ireland, Tentmaker Publications, 1995), p. 189.
10. M. Wilcock, *The Message of Psalms 1–72* (Leicester, England, IVP, 2001), p. 103.
11. Kidner, op. cit., p. 126.
12. D. Dickson, *Psalms* (London, England, Banner of Truth, 1965), p. 151.
13. The whole story is told in Jones, op. cit., p. 55.
14. See J. M. Boice, *Genesis* (Grand Rapids, USA, Baker, 1998), vol. 1, pp. 356ff.
15. From the hymn by Josiah Conder.
16. *The Poetical Works of Isaac Watts* (London, C. A. Cooke, 1796), p. 53.